Family Therapy

Christian Perspectives

Edited by

Hendrika Vande Kemp

BAKER BOOK HOUSE
Grand Rapids, Michigan 49516

Printed in the United States of America

Library of Congress Cataloging-in-Publication Data

Family therapy: Christian perspectives / edited by Hendrika Vande Kemp
p. cm.
Includes index.
ISBN 0-8010-9313-9
1. Family—Religious life. 2. Family psychotherapy.
I. Vande Kemp, Hendrika.
BV4526.2.F34   1991
259'.1—dc20
91-21803
CIP

To
all the students at Fuller Theological Seminary

who have rewarded my teaching of family therapy
and psychology of the family with enthusiasm
and made it an experience of joy,
plunged me headfirst into the deep waters of family process
research, and dared to ask the tough questions
which this volume seeks to answer.

Contents

Abbreviations

AB	Amplified Bible
AFTA	American Family Therapy Association
art.	article(s)
chap.	chapter
CRC	Christian Reformed Church
NIV	New International Version
RCA	Reformed Church in America
RLT	Relational Life Tasks
RSV	Revised Standard Version
TEV	Today's English Version

Introduction to the Series

Christian Explorations in Psychology is a series of books designed to explore the interface of contemporary psychology and Christianity. All the volumes in the series are intended for those in the field of psychology (either the upper-level undergraduate, graduate student, or professional) as well as those thoughtful Christians who have interest in issues in psychology and a desire to examine those from a Christian perspective. Each volume presents a scholarly treatment of the issues in one field of psychology; future volumes in the series will address such matters as epistemological and methodological aspects of psychological research and practice, cognitive psychology, family therapy, death and dying, psychotherapy and culture, and personality theory. It is hoped that these volumes may make a significant contribution to the ongoing dialogue between psychology and Christian theology, a dialogue which has often been better developed at the level of popular and journal article length works and is somewhat deficient in book-length treatments of a more scholarly sort.

David G. Benner
Hendrika Vande Kemp
Series Editors

Contributors

Alvin C. Dueck is associate professor of pastoral counseling at Mennonite Brethren Biblical Seminary, Fresno, California, where he is also the director of the marriage and family counseling program. A psychologist, Dueck holds a Ph.D. from Stanford University; he has done postdoctoral work in theology and family therapy at Notre Dame University, Yale University, and Heidelberg University. He is also a licensed psychologist.

Clarence Hibbs is professor of psychology at Pepperdine University, Malibu, California. He is active in the American Family Therapy Association, the American Association for Marriage and Family Therapy, and the California Association of Marriage and Family Therapists. Hibbs has worked extensively with the families of Pepperdine law students in creating preventive mental health programs. His Ph.D. is from the University of Iowa.

Austin J. Joyce is an ordained Presbyterian minister, a supervisory member of the American Association of Marriage and Family Therapy, and a supervisory member of the Center for Contextual Therapy (King of Prussia, Pennsylvania). He is also the director of the Institute for Male Studies, where he works with individuals, couples, and families in his clinical practice. He is co-author of *Truth and Trust in Contextual Therapy: Mastering*

11

Direct Address. His M.Div. is from Princeton Thelogical Seminary and his D. Min. is from Colgate Rochester BHC Seminary.

Barbara R. Krasner is director of the Center for Contextual Family Therapy and Allied Studies (King of Prussia, Pennsylvania) and the coauthor of *Between Give and Take: A Clinical Guide to Contextual Therapy.* She holds a Ph.D. from Temple University.

G. Peter Schreck is professor of pastoral care and counseling at Eastern Baptist Theological Seminary, Philadelphia, Pennsylvania. He has degrees in theology from Gordon-Conwell Theological Seminary and Princeton Theological Seminary. His degree in clinical psychology is from the Graduate School of Psychology, Fuller Theological Seminary. In addition to teaching, Schreck maintains a private practice as a marriage and family therapist.

Hendrika Vande Kemp is professor of psychology in the Graduate School of Psychology at Fuller Theological Seminary, Pasadena, California. She was the primary editor of *Psychology and Theology in Western Thought, 1672–1965* and is the author of more than 20 journal articles. Vande Kemp is active in the American Psychological Association, particularly Division 36 (Psychologists Interested in Religious Issues) and Division 26 (History of Psychology). Her Ph.D. is from the University of Massachusetts at Amherst.

Jon L. Yost is chaplain for the Center for Mental Health at the SwedishAmerican Hospital in Rockford, Illinois. He is also a licensed clinical social worker and a charter member of the American Family Therapy Association. Yost holds an M.Div. from Fuller Theological Seminary and an M.A. in social work from Indiana University.

Introduction

Family therapists are, in general, no more sensitive to religious issues than are other psychotherapists. The exceptions to this rule will emerge in the citations in the six chapters that follow. This volume arose out of a deeply felt need by the editor and contributors to add a new dimension to the family therapy literature. Each of the contributors has a strong commitment to the Judeo-Christian tradition, yet each represents a different segment of it. Jon Yost, himself a Presbyterian rooted in the Moravian tradition, writes about the solid Lutheranism of Christian F. Midelfort, a pioneer in Christian family therapy. Hendrika Vande Kemp, now a Presbyterian, anchors her analysis in the Reformed tradition as manifested primarily in her roots in the Christian Reformed Church. G. Peter Schreck speaks from the Baptist tradition; Clarence Hibbs, from the Church of Christ. As Barbara Krasner and Austin Joyce explore the pain of a Catholic family, they speak with a voice in which assumptions from both Judaism and Christianity are implicit. Finally, Alvin Dueck adds the unique perspective of the Mennonite tradition.

All the chapters also present a multigenerational perspective, consistent with the strong biblical emphasis on the legacy passing from parents to children, generation after generation. In Midelfort's model, the family therapist assesses the functioning of the following levels, which are listed in the order of importance: religious/philosophical, ethnic/cultural, psychological/emotional, social, and physical/biological. Thus, Midelfort not only recognized the importance of the religious and ethnic dimensions, but he did so long before their importance occurred to his professional peers. He stressed the role of reconciliation, of love and acceptance, as healing forces and also emphasized the role of the Eucharist and other "means of grace." Through Jon Yost's tribute, one senses that Midelfort was a teacher whose influence Yost will never forget, and we learn something of the therapeutic approach used by Yost himself.

In her chapter, Hendrika Vande Kemp illustrates how the family's religion can be included in every dimension of family assessment. Using the systems model of David Kantor and William Lehr, along with material on family development, she focuses on the access dimensions of space, time, and energy and the target dimensions of affect, power, and meaning. We catch in her work a personal glimpse of Dutch Christian Reformed families in the Midwest, in contrast to the Norwegian-American Lutheran families of Midelfort and Yost. Vande Kemp begins with the systemic assumption that the family is the matrix of identity and demonstrates that her religious subculture was a powerful matrix of a sometimes confused identity.

Peter Schreck addresses himself to the concerns of identity, intimacy, industry, and integrity, presenting a developmental framework of relational life tasks inspired by (but transforming) the theology of Helmut Thielicke as well as the psychologies of Erik Erikson, Daniel Levinson, and the developmental family theorists. The relational life tasks involve gaining self, sharing self, investing self, and saving self. Thus, Schreck casts the family dimensions of the two preceding chapters in a new form. Suddenly we see the family dimensions from a new angle that reveals hidden facets of individual and family development (regarded as a cybernetic "working out" rather than a linear unfolding) and shows the qualitative impact of spirituality on all of the dimensions of the family. He further explores the connection between the relational life tasks and the theological "moments" of creation, incarnation, redemption, and the kingdom of God. In Schreck's contribution we have an excellent model for bringing together psychological and theological perspectives on developing personhood in the context of the family.

Clarence Hibbs achieves a dual purpose in his chapter. First, he introduces and clarifies the four major dimensions of contextual family theory and therapy: facts, individual psychology, systems of transactional patterns, and relational ethics. Next, he applies these to the understanding of numerous aspects of congregational life, teasing out the subtle forces that contribute to schism and conflict as well as those that enable love, forgiveness, and service. Hibbs demonstrates that if the church is to be understood as the "family of God," an understanding of its dynamics must incorporate the wisdom of family theory. Hibbs offers a model that relies directly on Scripture and a wide range of systemic family theories, building into contextual family theory the missing Christian dimension. He also clearly spells out that his perspective offers a direct challenge to the individualism of contemporary American society and most practitioners in the helping profession.

The chapters by Schreck and Hibbs serve as an introduction to the chapter by Barbara Krasner and Austin Joyce, who develop in depth the interpersonal, transgenerational nature of being itself, thereby extending the contextual family theory of Ivan Boszormenyi-Nagy to which Krasner has already contributed extensively. Krasner's and Joyce's integration relies heavily on the philosophical theology of Martin Buber, which has components of both Judaism and existentialism. These authors emphasize that meaning itself is relational and discuss the role of justice, fair consideration, direct address, and ethical imagination as strategic components of relational ethics. For people who wonder about how a faith stance makes a difference in our day-to-day lives, this is an illuminating chapter. It has the flavor of a clinical case with commentary. Krasner's and Joyce's theme is about the integration of polar opposites mandated by the Judeo-Christian tradition. We recognize the all-too-familiar gap between religious ideals and actual living. We catch a glimpse of a family unaware of its trust base and the resources among them even in the midst of injury and estrangement. This is a family where healing might emerge in a co-creative process: repentance (each member's willingness to turn and face one another with the intention of reworking his or her own hurtful stance) and redemption (each member's willingness to say what he or she needs and wants and can offer in return) converge here to point a way toward healing through meeting.

In the final chapter by Alvin Dueck, the scope of ethics extends beyond the family, giving ethics political, communal, and historical components. Another dimension of family therapy emerges as Dueck explores its metaphors (formism, mechanism, contextualism, and organicism), models (preindustrial versus modern and postmodern), paradigms (the implicit ethical paradigm of contextual family theory), and stories (the reign of God as the story which shapes all our Christian thinking). Throughout his chapter, Dueck utilizes the insights of feminist critiques and adds his own appraisals rooted in the biblical story of the reign of God and his theological Anabaptist perspective. Dueck reveals the many layers of ethical assumptions that impinge on the family therapist, each level requiring self-examination and honest self-evaluation before Christian perspectives can emerge.

It is our hope that these Christian explorations in family therapy will meet at least some of the need for integration in the growing area of family theory and practice and that they will raise enough questions to generate even more creative integrative thinking.

1

Religion and Ethnicity in the Thought of Christian Fredrik Midelfort

Jon L. Yost

... a remarkable family therapist, a seminal thinker, a devoted teacher, and a spirited Christian.

—Jon L. Yost,
"For God, Country, and Family"

$\mathbb{C}$hristian Fredrik Midelfort, M.D., or "Fritz" as those who knew him would say, was one of the pioneers in family therapy. Indeed, he has been called the first Christian family therapist. Although he would shun such talk, the appellation befits him. Midelfort (1906–1984) began treating families in 1946 (Midelfort and Midelfort 1982)—the family stayed with the hospitalized patient in the Gunderson Clinic located in La Crosse, Wisconsin. He wrote the first book on family therapy, entitled

Portions of this chapter are based on a paper of the same title presented at the annual meeting of the American Family Therapy Association (AFTA) in San Diego, June 1985. An abstract of this paper was published in the *AFTA Newsletter* (Summer 1986): 16.

The Family in Psychotherapy (1957), and contributed to the first issue of *Family Process* (1962). Unique among Midelfort's contributions was his emphasis on the primacy of religion and ethnicity (in that order) in shaping family living over many generations (Midelfort 1980; Midelfort and Midelfort 1982).

This chapter will describe Midelfort's contributions to family therapy, provide an overview of his thinking, and state his theoretical perspective. Since we were associated for 7 years and together provided family consultation to many families and therapists, and spent hundreds of hours in conversation, much of what is written here has been taken from those experiences. I spent those many hours hearing firsthand his thinking—probing it, debating it, learning it. Midelfort was, in fact, my most valued mentor. I was often in his home in La Crosse, Wisconsin—a little bit of Norway he called it—nestled in Ebner's Coulee and replete with his Norwegian Lutheran family's artifacts. Many times he was in my home, which was dotted here and there with remembrances of my German-English Moravian-Presbyterian ancestry. One of my seminary professors once said there are two kinds of teachers: those who are creators of thought and new ideas and those who faithfully teach the ideas of others. It is my intent in this chapter to teach the ideas of Christian Fredrik Midelfort.

Midelfort's Family History

Midelfort was born on 23 October 1906 in Eau Claire, Wisconsin, and was one of 2 boys in a family with 11 children. He was of Norwegian and Lutheran descent; these factors, ethnicity and religion, were to become the dominant features of his outlook, his work, and his teaching. He left home at the age of 13 to attend a Reformed academy in Mercersberg, Pennsylvania, where his older brother was a student. Midelfort's father felt the schools in Eau Claire were not sophisticated enough to give his boys the education he wanted them to have. From these beginnings, Midelfort went on to study at Yale, Harvard, Cornell, Johns Hopkins (where he studied under Adolf Meyer, the eminent psychiatrist), and the University of Wisconsin (where Midelfort later also taught). He became board certified in internal medicine, neurology, and psychiatry, entering upon his residency in psychiatry at age 40. As a theologian, Midelfort was self-taught, and for 20 years he conducted a seminar at the

Lutheran Seminary in Minneapolis, Minnesota, on the relationship of religion to mental health and psychiatry.

The accomplishments of C. F. Midelfort in the field of family therapy were many. He published the first book on family therapy (1957), contributed a paper to the first issue of *Family Process* (1962), and was a member of renowned organizations, including the World Association of Social Psychiatry, the Pan American Medical Association, the American Family Therapy Association, and the American Society of Social Psychiatry. A partial listing of Midelfort's other affiliations reveals the breadth of his interests: he was a fellow in the American Medical Association and the American Psychiatric Association and a member of the Colloquium of the International Society of Psychiatrists, the Anthropes Society of Greece on Family Therapy, and the Christian Medical Society of the World Council of Churches.

Midelfort studied religion and culture—both present and historical—on a worldwide basis. Gifted and with an intense desire to learn, he traveled and read and talked with others in order to determine what was of value in helping families to a better life. He never founded a school of family therapy, choosing rather to live in La Crosse, where he saw more than 5,000 families over a period of 35 years (Yost 1980). Some of these he followed in his practice for three generations. Midelfort lamented that, in contrast to his own experience, many family therapists moved around a great deal, a circumstance that rendered continuity of care impossible and that kept the therapists from readily realizing the value he found in observing the multigenerational process with families. Proud of his Norwegian and Lutheran heritage, which he could trace to A.D. 1200, Midelfort delighted in his own family. He cherished his wife, their five children, and their families.

The Influence of Adolf Meyer

Midelfort's work provides a link with an eminent teacher of psychiatry, Adolf Meyer. In fact, there is a remarkable correspondence between Midelfort's thought and that of Meyer, which is not to say that Midelfort merely echoed his teacher. He added to, refined, and carried forward some of Meyer's ideas into a practice of family therapy that was modified in

order to reflect Midelfort's own Christian faith and his respect
for all religions of humankind.

Midelfort emphasized *ethnicity* as the vehicle by which traditions in the family are passed from generation to generation.
Earlier Adolf Meyer had written:

> The family is the nest in and around which the basic devel-
> opment of the character formation needed for certain levels of
> civilization seeks its best chance to take shape. Through similar
> tastes and yet enough mixtures of traits, family formation fur-
> nishes to the siblings and the parents and the relatives the
> familial combination of ties and opportunities, a school and test
> of affection, of tolerance, of cohesion.
>
> Within the relative intimacy of the *family group* and its
> radius of friendly and neighborly contacts, personal lives and
> their goals and standards can shape themselves better than in
> any other promiscuous group or one not based on blood relation-
> ship. (1948, 520; Meyer's italics)

Meyer concluded that "what is needed is a study of more of the
successful families and the conditions at work in them" (520).
These words—penned in 1930!—were later to reflect that
Midelfort was an ardent pupil, and he would weave these seminal ideas into his life, his work, and his own systems theory.

Midelfort used the word *systems* to communicate a key concept in his work: "We know that any change in one subsystem
affects all the others, and we also know there is a strong tendency for the total system to return to an equilibrium such as
existed before the change was introduced" (1980, 16). He consistently applied such terminology to descriptions of his practice methodology and insisted in his teaching on having a strong
theoretical base.[1] He taught that there are *levels* within the
family system which represent the *subsystems*, a conceptualization that resonates with Meyer: "While we might speak of a
hierarch[y] of sciences, there is no distinction between high and
low but only a logical grouping and grading according to the
temporary and other importance of the specific questions under
consideration" (1948, 602). Midelfort, following Meyer, had de-

---

1. Midelfort once mused that "Murray Bowen is said to be the only family
therapist given credit by some for having a theory of family functioning" and
added, "I think there may be others who do, too."

duced that one could speak of levels in a dynamic system as a way of denoting interacting influences and separable concerns.

Toward a Theory of Family Functioning

Midelfort described the family system as having five different levels from which functioning could take place. The level functioning in a particular family is called the *macrosystem*. This classification distinguishes the functioning level from the others and signifies its importance, indicating the perspective from which the family functions. The levels, which are listed in order of importance, are identified as follows:

1. Religious/philosophical
2. Ethnic/cultural
3. Psychological/emotional
4. Social
5. Physical/biological

Of greatest importance, the religious/philosophical is called the *decider level*, which guides the family's life decisions and most influences its overall functioning (Yost 1986).

When any one of the subsystems or levels is brought into play over the others, it is classified as the macrosystem. Identifying the macrosystem in operation in a family is one task of the therapist at the time of assessment. Further, it is incumbent upon the therapist to enter the macrosystem, for not only does it represent the level from which the family is functioning, but the macrosystem is also the level most accessible to the therapist. To enter elsewhere not only does an injustice to the family and its concerns and struggle but also means that the therapist might "misdiagnose" and lose the opportunity to help the family.

Midelfort held that all five delineated subsystems exist in a given family and that functional aspects of the family's system may be found among these subsystems. When dysfunction occurs, it is due to a conflict between two subsystems or, at least, to an emphasis on one to the exclusion of another. By no means is the individual lost or de-emphasized in this formulation. In fact, the clinical examples cited in Midelfort's writings demonstrate that his theoretical formulations give the individual his or her place of prominence in the system. The therapist's task is not to force conformity but to show the family how the individual's behavior may be pointing either to something that needs to be changed in the system or to something that is in need of being restored or emphasized. The goal of therapy then is to bring the conflicting subsystems back into harmony with one another by building on the positives that exist in the family. In a functional family, the levels or subsystems are in balance. When they are out of balance, dysfunction may occur; for example,

> where ethnic and religious systems are the macrosystem that controls the family's activities, there is a lack of individuation. This is present in rural areas where one ethnic tradition, one religious denomination, one type of work, farming, and one place of residence, the farm, all are integrated around the church and social life of the community. For example, this is true of Norwegian American Lutheran farmers who have lived on the same or neighboring farms since their ancestors first came over from Norway. (Midelfort 1980, 16)

The family makes its own decision as to the level from which it operates. This decision may be more or less in the awareness of the family. For the therapist it is critical to discern the operational level so as to gain acceptance by the family and to not do violence to its traditions; at the same time, the therapist must probe within the family to find an improved level of functioning. While Midelfort regarded the religious and ethnic subsystems as being of the greatest importance, he recognized that conformity to them in the family in a slavish manner could lead to dysfunction: "The depressed family makes ethnic and religious systems their top priority and all the subsystems are expected to conform to this" (Midelfort 1980, 20). Midelfort made this statement in the context of the rural Norwegian-American Lutheran families he treated in his practice, but he believed it would transfer outside the region to wherever a predominant ethnic/religious tradition prevailed in a given family. As a word of caution, he noted that "the dominance of a macrosystem made up of history and religion can be harmful, as can their absence" (18).

According to Midelfort, the absence of a strong bond of ethnic/religious tradition does not preclude the family's functional stability; however, the family must depend on another level of functioning for its well-being. In reviewing one family, Midelfort concluded that

> there was instability in all systems in this family. Their mixed ethnic background and changing religious affiliation gave their historical and cultural systems no strength or continuity. There was difficulty at the biological level, especially during pregnancies. They moved from farm to farm but continued their occupation as farmers. This [the social level] was the only stable system they had and because of this they were able to keep going and regain balance and equilibrium after shocks had disrupted their family life. (1980, 21)

While Midelfort emphasized the importance of the religious and ethnic levels, he believed a balance in perspective had to be maintained: "There is no intention of saying that the ethnic and religious systems alone play a deciding role in family health or illness. All the levels are involved but in the hierarchy of levels the ethnic and religious are the highest" (21).

Family Assessment and Functioning

Midelfort was guided in his work with a family by an assessment formulation that elicited a comprehensive overview of the family's spiritual history. By using the assessment outline, which has not been published heretofore, Midelfort was able to determine the family's functioning.

Spiritual History and Examination

Present Difficulty

Chief complaint and the setting in which it has developed. What factors have influenced it; the environmental influences (such as social, cultural, education, physical, mental, and ecclesiastical factors).

Past History

Year of birth, place of birth, and number of brothers and sisters.

Father: Nationality, church (pastor), occupation, health (spiritual, physical, and mental), relationship with father.

Mother: Natioality, church (pastor), occupation, health, relationship with mother.

Siblings in order, such as:
  Brother—spouse, church (pastor), children, occupation, church attendance, residence.
  Sister—same as for *brother*.

School: How far he/she went and at what age.

Religious school: Confirmation, attendance, and support of church.

Spiritual Examination

Appearance, neatness, gestures, facial expression, restlessness, speech, mood.

[Then he turned to his Christian allegiance and, where this coincided with the faith of the family, followed a trinitarian formulation.]

God the Father: Authority, attitudes, and the feelings toward the role of obedience. What is the will of God? God as Creator. First article of the Apostles' Creed.

God the Son: Brotherhood, compassion, feelings, and ideas about redemption.

God the Holy Spirit: Creativity, unity, becoming a person, spirits or mood, sleep, appetite, weight, sex life, worries, spells, fears, anxieties, sense of reality, voices, tongues, demons.

Personality: Temper, grudges, sociability, perfectionism, sensitivity, shyness, inferiority, self-consciousness.

Diagnostic Formulation

  Type of problem
  Background history
  Need for change
  Plans for changing

In its barest form, Midelfort's assessment outline reflects not only his Christian perspective but also the rural area (Norwegian-American and Lutheran at its foundation) from which he came and in which he practiced. The formulation also reveals the dominant theme of Midelfort's work, namely, the primacy of religion and ethnicity in the family functioning and their significance as the key to the family's essential well-being.

Midelfort was strongly influenced by what his teacher had stated regarding the role of religion in individual and group life: "Individual and group psychiatry has taught us [to deal] with individual wholes and group wholes [emphasizing the role of] religion as a way of trust and reciprocal obligations as well as dependabilities in life" (Meyer 1948, 624). Following his teacher, Midelfort concluded:

> Of the several systems that structure and organize the family, the ethnic and religious are of particular importance where the past is held in the highest esteem. Cohesiveness, conformity and continuity help create a community in which there is a hierarchy with God, the Father at the top, followed by the king [a doff of the Norwegian hat], the pastor, the family's father and mother. In this situation the culture is responsible for the structure of the family and the other subsystems fall into line serving the macrosystem, especially its religious and ethnic components. (1980, 16)

Midelfort's sentiment regarding the primacy of religion and its corollary, ethnicity, may be summed up by his teacher, who wrote that "psychiatry gives us also a new appreciation of the religious life and needs of our race. Man's religion shows in his capacity to feel and grasp his relations and responsibility toward the largest unit or force he can conceive, and his capacity for faith and hope in a deeper and more lasting interdependence of individual and race with the Ruler or rules of the universe" (Meyer 1948, 13).

Toward a Theology of Family Functioning

Recurrent themes pertaining to Christian beliefs and practices surface as one studies Midelfort's *The Family in Psychotherapy* (1957). It was in fact the "first book" in family therapy.[2] This primary and pioneering source of family therapy theory and practice merits study by family theoreticians and practitioners. A careful study of the examples and concepts in this book brings

2. Midelfort told me of meeting Nathan Ackerman in New York and saying to him, "You wrote the first book in family therapy." Ackerman replied, "No. Yours was first. Mine was the second" (Yost 1986, 151). Ackerman's *Psychodynamics of Family Life: Diagnosis and Treatment of Family Relationships* (New York: Basic Books) was published in 1958.

into focus the reality that much of what Midelfort did has its basis in Christian commitment and belief. A strong faith in God and in the power of tradition through many generations led Midelfort to conclude that certain beliefs important to the family, when stimulated by the therapist, brought healing. Healing, of course, is integral to the gospel itself and is a primary goal of the physician and therapist, as it was for Jesus and his disciples. The central concepts in Midelfort's book include love, acceptance, understanding, forgiveness, grace, and human contact, of which the latter is especially important in establishing the others, with regard to the family in its interactions among its members. This emphasis shifted the focus from the therapist and his or her impact on the family toward the family's bringing about its own well-being by directing attention to the healing inherent in its own traditions and to connecting with one another.

The primacy of physical contact in establishing a therapeutic bond was brought to my attention in an instant when Midelfort related to me its role in the Norwegian tradition. He pointed out that upon greeting a family he always shook hands with each family member. To neglect to do so, he reported, was perceived by the Norwegian family as rejection. Midelfort transferred this cultural perception to each family we saw together. By the simple act of shaking hands, he intended to communicate love and acceptance and, in a manner of speaking, the urge for reconciliation among the alienated—whether between family members or within a family member struggling with himself or herself to be whole again.

A most powerful manifestation of Midelfort's healing touch occurred when Midelfort and I visited an Amish family in Wisconsin. Knowing the Amish to be insular, we found ourselves traveling back country roads in search of a family we had met earlier, when the daughter was hospitalized with an eating disorder. On the occasion of our meeting, the father had invited us to their home and had given us explicit directions on how to find their farm, should we ever travel their way. Arriving at the home, Midelfort and I were welcomed in and found ourselves accepted by the parents and other family members as bearers of hope for a troubled household.[3] The two of us brought knowl-

3. I was reminded of stories Midelfort told me of traveling to similar, albeit non-Amish, homes with his father, who himself was a physician in rural Wisconsin.

edge of aspects of physical and mental health and a theology informed by Christian traditions, Protestant and Reformed, as found in Lutheran, Moravian, and Presbyterian formulations. The family had its own traditions, Christian and Amish. Together with that family, Midelfort and I had one goal: the effecting of mutual acceptance, the communication of love, and the achievement of reconciliation. Since this was the only contact we had in the home, the outcome of this visit cannot be measured or known. In relating the experience, my intent is not to report the outcome, but to convey a Gestalt. It is this kind of attunement that Midelfort sought to establish in his practice and which is the essence of the case histories he portrays in his book and other writings.

As a therapist with certification in psychiatry, internal medicine, and neurology, Midelfort brought to bear all his training in his efforts to heal. In working with families, he was informed by conventional diagnostic formulations. His book deals with schizophrenia, depression, paranoid illness, psychopathic personality (including character neuroses), and psychoneuroses. At the same time, he recognized the limitations of any nosology since, as he was fond of saying, "the thing named and the thing itself are not the same thing." By this he apparently intended to convey that formulations were not in and of themselves the royal road to recovery. In fact, Midelfort wrote as follows regarding the treatment of depression: "The flow of life through receiving and giving love, through becoming aware of being cared for, and objectifying this feeling in acts of friendship with others once more is begun, and the depression is over" (1957, 104).

The "flow of life" is what is important to any Christian formulation based on "receiving and giving love." Though it is not the exclusive property of the Christian therapist, the love is for the Christian therapist the sine qua non of performance and practice. It constitutes what cannot be taught formally, what surely is in the Christian's province to communicate whether working with an avowedly Christian family or not, and what Midelfort so effectively communicated in his practice. He embodied in his teaching and practice the importance of the use of self, not only in human contact but also in how he sought to be perceived and accepted by the family (Midelfort 1982).

By way of further example, a recounting of Midelfort's methodology in interviewing families is instructive. He repeatedly stated that much could be done, which was currently not being attained, by interviewing the families of hospitalized family members in the presence of the treatment team. To those who thought the cost factor too high to formalize such practice, Midelfort countered that in fact it had cost-saving features. He held that when all members of the treatment team were allowed to participate, they potentially could arrive more quickly at conclusions that would facilitate reuniting the one hospitalized with those family members outside the hospital.

Based on extensive experience, Midelfort's view was born in part out of the frustration of trying to teach the value of family therapy to others and, on the more positive side, from his belief in the benefits of using the expertise of every discipline involved to help solve the family's difficulties and improve functioning. Midelfort wrote that "in family consultations, with patient, relative, and therapist present, the combined good will, potential creativeness, love, and affection of the group provide the motive for that interest and devotion that are needed for those actions that relate objects and persons together in movements that satisfy cultural, social, and individual drives in an integrated way" (1957, 17). Further expression of his view is found in the same work: "By bringing the family and patient together in interviews . . . the family unity is strengthened. . . . In this way the family takes part in creating something that is beautiful and has depth of value and meaning for both the patient and relative" (19–20).

In recounting the activities of Midelfort with families and hospital team staff, the following scene emerges:

Fritz's interview plan was one of the most thoughtful and artful I have ever witnessed. Our consultations always included the principal therapist and other interested professional health care providers, e.g., nurses, pastors, social workers, other health care providers, doctors, and on occasion, a hospital administrator who was interested in our work. It did not matter to Fritz whether the entire family could be present. He would say, "We begin with whoever is willing to be present. The others may follow in another session. Our task is to help the patient, and those interested, with the family's problem." His first task would be to have each person identify himself or herself, including each staff person present. He would explain that we were all here to learn, including himself, and to help. Almost invariably he would begin the family interview with the "identified patient." After having the patient, however briefly or simply, disclose his or her distress, he would in turn include other family members, making quite sure not to render judgments of any kind. Staff present were not there to observe but to contribute. Each was included fully as a member of the team, and each was present to learn and to assist in the alleviation of the problem. However problematic the family's situation, Fritz always found and highlighted the positives present in the family. These became then the basis for hope and the desired progress. (Yost 1986, 150)

In this descriptive account a conceptualization fundamental to a Christian definition of family therapy is present, namely, love and acceptance directed toward reconciliation within the context of community.

Ethnicity and Religion

Midelfort taught that where there is a mixture of ethnic and religious traditions, the family should be helped to identify the one that they feel most attracted toward and build on a knowledge of that tradition. Where religious traditions are mixed, he indicated that the more diverse or dissimilar those traditions are, the more likely the result would be, to use his word, "nothing." By this he meant that, in the effort to minimize the diversity, all religious traditions and beliefs are given up and what results is a philosophy. What is thereafter communicated in the family may be termed *values* rather than *beliefs*, which one associates with religion.

Most of Midelfort's work, it must be remembered, was with rural Norwegian-American Lutheran families. This, however, does not preclude extrapolating from the clinical examples he gives what is important in working with families of any religious/ethnic tradition. Further, in his work Midelfort was acutely aware of the direct correspondence in tradition between himself and the families and the primacy of this correspondence in effectively treating them: "The common bond between the therapist and this family was their joint Norwegian Lutheranism. The psychiatrist and father spoke together in Norwegian, and this cultural value, with its potent emotional

overtones, helped create a security and confidence in the therapeutic program" (Midelfort 1957, 41). Though a correspondence of religious/ethnic tradition between the therapist and
family may be advantageous, the correspondence is not requi-
site for their work together to be effective. However, the therapist from a different religious/ethnic tradition must be cognizant of the family's traditions in both spheres and must elicit
from the family what is important to them, before proceeding
with any treatment; "family systems theory shows us that the
therapist can enter the family at any systems level, be it religious, cultural, social, psychological, or physical, and influence
the other levels" (Midelfort and Midelfort 1982, 448).

In a chapter Midelfort wrote with his daughter (1982), they
delineate aspects of ethnic and religious tradition that the therapist should take into account. It is instructive to consider
these and then translate them to other ethnic and religious traditions. Foremost among these considerations is the therapist's
developing a knowledge of the history of the ethnic group
involved. Some of this can be gained from formal histories of a
people and their culture. For this, the *Harvard Encyclopedia of
American Ethnic Groups* (Thernstrom, Orlov, and Handlin
1980) is useful. But other important features can only be
gained by either being a part of that tradition or careful listening to members of a particular ethnic group recount what cannot be found in formal writings about that group. This may be
termed the *folk history,* or that which is part of oral tradition.
What is important here is not the accuracy of detail that family
members recount but the fact that they base their functioning
at least in part on what has been passed down over the generations.

When an ethnic group has a particular religious expression
attached to it, knowledge of that religious belief system becomes
as important as knowledge of the ethnic or cultural tradition.
In writing about the Norwegian-American Lutheran tradition,
the Midelforts note that "Lutheranism emphasized the individual's responsibility in dealing with the supernatural" (1982,
439). Translated into behavior, this responsibility meant that
"among the religious, ill health is seen as resulting from lack of
faith. It is either a punishment for sins or a test of their belief"
(443). From the theological perspective of Lutheranism, dualism found expression in the opposites of God/devil, grace/sin,

and forgiveness/guilt. Midelfort dealt with these opposites as realities as he functioned as an advocate for the family in its struggle to find a more constructive life (Midelfort and Midelfort 1982; personal conversation, January 1980).

In addition to the history and theology pertaining to a particular ethnic/religious tradition, the therapist should be knowledgeable about other areas as well. These include attitudes toward accepting help from outside the family. The Midelforts note that among Norwegian-Americans "asking directly for help is uncommon" (1982, 441). An attitude such as this becomes an important consideration with members of any ethnic group as the therapist attempts to engage them in treatment. The therapist must also be aware of nonverbal aspects of behavior. For example, the Midelforts observed that among Norwegian-Americans "friendship is demonstrated through loyalty over time and by spending time together not by sharing intimate problems" (443).

Another important aspect of relationships is sexual involvement. In this, as in other areas, critical errors can be made if the therapist is not informed as to its place in a particular ethnic tradition. According to the Midelforts, "sexual activity is an acceptable but strictly private concern and is not openly discussed" (1982, 442) in Norwegian-American families. With this knowledge, the Midelforts caution that "in a therapeutic situation it is not advisable to approach the question of sexuality too early, and it should not be brought up at all if children are present" (442–43).

Music and art also are to be studied as sources of information regarding an ethnic tradition (Midelfort and Midelfort 1982, 444). And one final area to be studied is food, which for the Norwegian-American is "invested with symbolic significance" (443), a concept Midelfort carried over into his theoretical perspective. He found that in the Christian sacrament of the Eucharist the symbolic, as represented by the bread and wine, and the biologic, as represented by the body and blood of Christ, become as one. To participate in the Eucharist is to bring about healing. Hence, Midelfort customarily asked the Christian family whether they partook and, if they did, what benefit they found in the sacrament. If they did not, he would inquire as to what kept them from participation. Midelfort did not hold that such participation contained magic, but rather that partaking of the sacrament invited healing and wholeness. The family was invited to use every available means along with the therapeutic effort to bring health to each subsystem level.

Above all else, Midelfort believed that the family contains the seeds of its own recovery and well-being: "Psychotherapy may well be described as the discovery of new options not initially remembered by the patient or family. These options, however, are already present as assets within the family and its cultural history" (Midelfort and Midelfort 1982, 448). In characteristic unassuming fashion, Midelfort reflected on the role of the therapist in assisting a family in finding its assets:

> The psychiatrist gives the patient the experience of being loved and supported by him in the present during each interview. . . . The role of the therapist to understand, accept, and love is different from that of members of the patient's family, in that they make demands on her to give them what they need from her, and these demands affect what they are able to give her, while the psychiatrist gives without needing, in his position and with his personality, to receive from her anything except what she can accomplish with her family in the objective reality of their life together. (1957, 54–55)

Two vignettes based on families with whom Midelfort and I consulted illustrate the application in therapy of the dimensions of religion and ethnicity. The first family was a young couple who came for consultation because the wife was severely depressed. She had recently delivered a boy with several minor birth anomalies. Following the birth, her depression became more severe. She had concluded that the infant's anomalies were evidence that God was punishing her for having an abortion when she was an adolescent. Her first pregnancy was by the man who eventually became her husband, but the two, by their own admission, were not ready to be married, let alone be parents. The couple was Italian Roman Catholic. This new infant, born some 10 years after the abortion, was their first child. We learned that over the years they had both discontinued going to mass. Upon inquiry we ascertained that she believed the church had excommunicated her because of the abortion. Now that they had a boy, they were eager to have him baptized in the Roman Catholic faith. The parents felt embarrassed and guilty about going to the priest, thinking they would not only have to tell him about the abortion but would also be judged for having done this. The abortion, they further reasoned, would lead to repercussions by the clerics of the church. With the couple's permission, Midelfort and I consulted with a Roman Catholic chaplain at the hospital. He informed us that the woman was not excommunicated and still had full access to the sacraments of the church. Although there were other family difficulties that had to be worked out, this information freed the couple to approach the local priest and have their son baptized. The process enabled them to begin work on their other issues in a more productive manner.

Another family who came for consultation had a member on the psychiatric service team. This family was German Lutheran. They were constantly fighting physically, and there had been several instances of serious injury. Midelfort and I asked that they have their pastor, whom we knew to be important to them, attend the session. He did this readily, as he had worked with them in the parish context for several years to no avail. When during the session the wife was asked by Midelfort about the fighting, she jumped up out of her chair, looked menacingly at Midelfort and then at her husband, and exclaimed, "Do you want me to show you how I hit him?" She had her fist clenched and drawn back ready to strike upon command. Neither Midelfort nor I was inclined to give such permission, and Midelfort calmly said, "No. Please sit down." She did, and the session continued in a relatively quiet state.

At one point, when the couple was being asked about their ethnic traditions in the home and their church participation and related matters of their faith, Midelfort inquired as to whether they took the Eucharist together. (This was his usual inquiry regarding the rituals of any faith tradition, that is, to ask if the family kept the religious rituals of their faith.) The couple said they did, and the pastor affirmed that they were in regular attendance. Midelfort then suggested that at the conclusion of the session the couple, the wife's mother, who was also present, and the pastor go to the hospital chapel and partake of the Eucharist together. They agreed, and after the session, they did. While this act did not end the family's difficulties, it brought calm into the session and prompted the members to agree to do the one thing they appeared to share, namely, the practicing of their faith and its traditions.

An astute observer of the human condition, Midelfort noted that when persons of the same religious and ethnic background marry, there is a tendency toward recurrent depressions, especially in rural areas. At the same time, a correspondence of ethnic and religious traditions tends to produce a harmony little found outside such a bond. Midelfort's conclusions were based on his experience with some 5,000 families in his practice over nearly 40 years. He added that a mixing of faith and ethnic traditions can lead to a denial of both religious traditions; however, along with this there may be a concomitant effort to keep alive at least the ethnic traditions. When in later years Midelfort began seeing families in the urban area of Chicago, Illinois, he observed that there appeared to be much more "character disordered" behavior, that is, more divorce, family violence, and generalized "acting out," in this population than in the families in the rural areas of Wisconsin. In reference to the urban families with such societally problematic behavior, Midelfort frequently pointed to the lack of continuity that seemed to result from such disparate mixtures of religious and ethnic traditions.

Contributions

In 1980, I conducted an interview, which was videotaped and later transcribed, with Midelfort. His own words from that interview are useful in assessing his contributions to family therapy theory and practice:

[My contribution,] first of all, [is in] taking families as experiments in nature, as Dr. Meyer had taught me, taking a history of attitudes and habits rather than looking for hidden, unconscious motivations. Second, coming to see problems in terms of religious, cultural, social, psychological, and physical difficulties. I was able to develop, through my training and experience, an ease with physical illness, with religious illness, with social illness, with psychological illness. My training has been broad enough to be able to make a survey of a family in a much broader way than I was taught in my residency or medical school training. I've specialized particularly in the study of ethnic or cultural religious factors as they play a role in the health and illness of families. I would say that may be part of the contribution. In addition, having families live in the hospital with the patient is another. I also wrote the first book on family therapy. (Yost 1980, 16)

As for the family staying with the patient in the hospital, Midelfort pioneered this effort, which grew out of his own medical training.

At Payne-Whitney in New York City . . . , the patients were upstairs in the upper floors and the families were seen on the first floor. The patient and the family were never seen together. When I came back to the Gunderson Clinic in La Crosse [Wisconsin] to practice, I decided to put the two together. I had the families stay in the hospital room with the patient on a 24-hour basis. These were psychiatric cases of all varieties and types. The family was there and was responsible. For example, the subcoma insulin therapy I was giving at the time [in 1946] was administered by the family to see that the proper degree of insulin reaction was not exceeded. The family was much better at it than the nurses. The family took part in whatever recreational or occupational therapy there was. They lived on the ward in a private room. The patients were mixed with all other patients and not just psychiatric patients. This was done deliberately because in some ways the hospital is the worst environment for psychiatric patients. They sit around together, compare notes, criticize their doctors or psychiatrists and aggravate their illnesses. Whereas when there are medical and surgical patients and families, they are exposed to "normalcy." And it is very beneficial. In a general hospital there were no locked doors or windows. Within 7 to 10 days it was possible to get them out of the hospital, even though they were hallucinating and deluded. There was much rapid improvement when the whole family was involved or at least certain members. One saw the illness in terms of what was going on in the family as the focus of attention.

. . . [After discharge,] they would come to see me in the outpatient clinic—the whole family—and we continued there. I have followed families for thirty years, so I know what's happening to them. The great blessing of staying in one place is to get to know the families. I have over 200 families out of the 5,000 that I saw during the 30-year period where I have seen more than one member of the family as patients at different times. I've gotten the story about the family from several people in the family, and I'm able to see what effect family therapy of this type has on long-term health. (Yost 1980, 13–14)

Midelfort used his professional expertise in all its dimensions. As an internist, neurologist, and psychiatrist, he could assess what was going on with the patient and put that behavior or symptomatology in the context of the family. To this Midelfort added the dimensions of religion and ethnicity, having become convinced that these played a crucial role in health and wholeness for the family and the individual. In studying religion and in considering its influence on family life, he accepted belief as integral to well-being and healing. He did not equate beliefs with values and saw the former as influencing the quality and health of interpersonal relationships and the latter only as derivatives from beliefs and not the substance of beliefs themselves. He, therefore, pointed to the primacy of religion as it is expressed in the context of one of humankind's most intimate associations, namely, the family.

Further, Midelfort illuminated family life by focusing on the importance of ethnic traditions in shaping the family for many generations. While he practiced primarily with Norwegian-Americans, he was informed about and conversant with many ethnic traditions. Being made aware of this important area, one can study these traditions and see how they are expressed in the context of any family in treatment. The therapist then is in the position of being instructed by the family as to the importance of its own traditions. The next step becomes helping the family to find its strengths and to build on them.

Midelfort's emphasis on "social psychiatry and cultural anthropology" (1957, vi) carried with it a corresponding absence of emphasis on conventional psychodynamic terminology and interpretation. In 1952 he presented what has been described as "probably the first paper on family therapy ever presented at a psychiatric convention in the United States" (Midelfort 1982, 1). In that presentation he did include psychodynamic terminology. However, a careful reading of that paper together with subsequent writings and our discussions indicate that fundamentally he remained loyal to the precepts of the social psychiatry and cultural anthropology that guided his work. He indicated that he took from Adolf Meyer terms like *more or less awareness* as replacements for concern about *conscious* or *unconscious* motivation.

Midelfort came to the family and the individual with a concern for their establishing their own perspective on health which was based on factors and influences they knew to be theirs. His practice with families was guided by an awareness of social interaction: "The use of relatives in the care of psychiatric patients is the outgrowth of a new theory which considers the family, not the individual, as the unit or organism in which illness occurs. . . . The family, therefore, must be viewed as the unit of treatment. Because relatives take part in treatment, the social organization and personality growth of the patient takes place in the familiar atmosphere of family experience" (Midelfort 1957, v). This emphasis on the "family experience" led to the practice previously mentioned, namely, that whenever possible, Midelfort would include representatives of other disciplines in the family session. This might be a social worker whom he saw as lending a perspective on the importance of the interrelatedness of systems or a pastor with his or her emphasis on the spiritual. In the hospital, the medical specialist or nurse would bring his or her own area of expertise to bear on the patient's medical problem and attendant care. By so organizing treatment resources, Midelfort concluded, not only would costs be lowered but a more accurate assessment of the family and its assets would be assured.

Midelfort saw that we are all players on the stage and that each must participate in a way that promotes the well-being of the other. Whether functioning is considered from the religious, ethnic, social, psychological, or physical levels, it is only when these are in balance that optimal performance is forthcoming.

References

Meyer, A. 1948. *The commonsense psychiatry of Dr. Adolf Meyer: Fifty-two selected papers.* New York: McGraw-Hill.

Midelfort, C. F. 1957. *The family in psychotherapy.* New York: McGraw-Hill.

———. 1962. Use of members of the family in the treatment of schizophrenia. *Family Process* 1:114–18.

———. 1980. Ethnic and religious factors in family illnesses. *Bulletin of the American Association for Social Psychiatry* 1, 3:16–21.

———. 1982. Use of family in the treatment of schizophrenic and psychopathic patients. *Journal of Marital and Family Therapy* 8:1–11.

Midelfort, C. F., and H. C. Midelfort. 1982. Norwegian families. In *Ethnicity and family therapy,* ed. M. McGoldrick, J. K. Pearce, and J. Giordano, 438–56. New York: Guilford Press.

Thernstrom, S., A. Orlov, and O. Handlin, eds. 1980. *Harvard encyclopedia of American ethnic groups.* Cambridge: Harvard University Press.

Yost, J. L. 1980. The legacy of a family therapy pioneer: C. F. Midelfort, M.D. Unpublished edited transcription of a videotaped interview recorded on January 23, 1980. Transcript in Yost's possession.

————. 1986. For God, country, and family: A personal tribute to Christian Fredrik Midelfort, M.D. *Family Process* 25:149–51.

2

The Family, Religion, and Identity

A Reformed Perspective

Hendrika Vande Kemp

Introduction

Q. 1. What is your only comfort, in life and in death?
A. That I belong—body and soul, in life and in death—not to myself but to my faithful Savior, Jesus Christ, . . . (Office of the General Assembly 1983, 4.001)

Thus begins the Heidelberg Catechism of 1563, the primary creed of the Gereformeerde Kerk (one of the Dutch Calvinist churches) and the Christian Reformed denomination (the CRC) which formed the faith of my childhood. The catechism consisted of 129 questions and answers, distributed over 52 Lord's

An earlier version of this chapter was written at the invitation of the Western Psychological Association for presentation at their annual meeting in Burlingame, California, 28 April–1 May 1988. That paper was also presented at Union Theological Seminary in New York on 23 February 1988 and at Bringham Young University, Provo, Utah, on 15 March 1990.

Days, designed to incorporate into the 52 Sundays of the year an annual review of the major articles of our faith. As a latency-aged child, I memorized the catechism and every Saturday morning attended classes clarifying its meaning. In adolescence these were replaced with additional homework and Wednesday-evening meetings of the young people's group, which doubled as a social network. These studies culminated on Palm Sunday of 1966 (a day well-remembered in our rural community because of a devastating tornado that damaged the church) in my public profession of faith, an adolescent rite of passage witnessed by my entire nuclear family and "the family of God," and shared with several peers.

In this sequence of events, familiar to millions of American Protestants, we see the essential interpenetration of religion, identity, and the family. The Heidelberg Catechism begins with a clear statement of *belongingness and identity*: I belong to Jesus Christ. It continues with an assertion of *separateness*: Christ "freed me from the dominion of the devil" (Office of the General Assembly 1983, 4.001). In the learning of the catechism, Wednesday evenings and Saturday mornings were defined as sacred time, and both were spent in a sacred place: the church building. In the remainder of the answer to the first question of the catechism are contained time present (the statement of identity), time past (the redeeming work of Jesus Christ), and time future (the assurance of eternal life).

What follows here is deeper exploration of this interpenetration of religion, identity, and the family. The organization of the material is based on the systems theory of David Kantor and William Lehr, as summarized in *Inside the Family* ([1975] 1976). Illustrations will be drawn primarily from my own experience. I was born in the Netherlands, the 8th of 10 children in a closely knit Gereformeerd family. At the age of eight, I became an immigrant, settling in southwestern Michigan after a trans-Atlantic journey that involved an "accident at sea" and an emergency stop to board another ocean liner in a French harbor. In Michigan our family became part of a rural community which was, for the most part, very welcoming and kind, but generally not religious. Our immediate religious community—a local congregation of the Christian Reformed Church— consisted primarily of third-generation (or older) Dutch families whose prejudices against "the Dutchmen" who had just "come over on the boat" were explicit and often cruel. This made adjustment exceedingly difficult: those who supported our religious values were threatened by our immigrant status; those indifferent to our immigrant status found it difficult to empathize with our religious stance. This painful cultural assimilation may account for elements of "religious pathology" in my own life, as it took me several decades to untangle the legitimate aspects of Calvinism from the prejudices of a Dutch community struggling with its feeling of cultural inferiority.

Access Dimensions

Kantor and Lehr's ([1975] 1976) systems theory focuses on six dimensions of the family. The *access* dimensions of *space, time,* and *energy* "describe and include the physical aspects of family members' quest for experience. They are the quantitative means through which members' need for safety and participation are actualized" (Kantor and Lehr [1975] 1976, 36). The *target* dimensions of *affect, power,* and *meaning* "describe and include the conceptual aspects of family members' quest for experience. They are the qualitative means through which members' need for specific goals are thematically actualized" (36). The basic assumption of Kantor and Lehr is that family members "gain access to targets of affect, power, and meaning through the way in which they and their families regulate the media of space, time, and energy" (37).

Space

There are two kinds of questions relating to the space dimension. First, how does a family "develop, defend, and maintain its system and subsystem territories? Second, how does it regulate distance among its own members?" (Kantor and Lehr [1975] 1976, 41). Kantor and Lehr describe three major methods of space maintenance—*bounding, linking,* and *centering*—each subdivided into several precise functions.

Bounding. Bounding is "the mechanism in which families establish and maintain their territory within the larger community space by regulating both incoming and outgoing traffic" (Kantor and Lehr [1975] 1976, 68). Through bounding, "members of a family decide what kinds of things are allowed to enter the family space and under what conditions, and what kinds of items are simply not permitted admission" (68). Bounding issues are issues of safety, protecting the family from external dangers. The subfunctions of bounding include *mapping, routing, screening,* and *patrolling.* The family "develops its own 'map,' or picture, of the exterior culture" (68), noting ways the culture resembles and differs from the family's subculture and distinguishing those persons and events which are safe from those which are dangerous. The map provides reference points by which new experiences can be tested, and may in turn be modified by those experiences. Family movements are then routed along "pathways designated and approved by the system map" (69). Families also screen "both incoming and outgoing traffic, permitting some people to pass and prohibiting others" (69). The screening checkpoints are enforced by the family's "border guards," who patrol the relevant perimeter points and oversee the traffic into and out of the family territory.

Bounding in our family involved making the distinction between non-Christians and Christians, and judging the latter by the rules of our particular Christian subculture. My friends in high school included Christians of many denominations, bound together by common involvement in Youth for Christ International. Yet I lost considerable social status since my Christian identity dictated that I not dance, smoke, drink, or see movies and the family's socioeconomic status ruled out many other extracurricular activities. With Calvinism defined in part by its break from Catholicism, I was surprised at the emergence of a close friendship with a Catholic, which forced me to challenge the prejudices of my faith and provided the first glimpse of sisterhood in Christ. I still have a paper I wrote as a high-school junior about this adventure in personal differentiation, yet my willingness to reveal this to an empathic writing teacher did not extend to sharing it with my family, whose disapproval I feared. I suspect that even now they are unaware of her place in my heart and her role in the initiation of a liberation process that in adulthood is manifested in an extended friendship network that includes a diversity of Protestants and Catholics; Jews; agnostics and atheists; and followers of nontraditional religions. None of these relationships challenges my relationship with God. Such challenges come not from the differing convictions of others, but from my personal experiences. And even these challenge my theology rather than my faith, a distinction often overlooked by those who emphasize reason rather than experience.

Linking. Linking regulates family distance, "the physical and conceptual associations and dissociations of all persons within the family's spatial interior" (Kantor and Lehr [1975] 1976, 70). Linking governs the family's interpersonal relations and focuses on family members and their movements around various targets. The linking subfunctions include *bridging, buffering, blocking out, channeling,* and *recognizing.* Bridging brings family members "into closer voluntary contact with one another or with objects" (71) and fosters both relatedness and efficacy. Its complement is buffering, "a maneuver in which different persons or persons and objects move farther apart or voluntarily separate" (71). Buffering includes such voluntary behaviors as dodging, escaping, avoiding, and distancing. Blocking out involves "coercive or involuntary separating of persons or persons and objects" (72). Often the involuntary component is covert, and "the person who has been blocked out in some way may feel terribly angry and frustrated, for [s]he does not share the blocker's view of the target bearer's need for protection" (72). Its complement is channeling, "the involuntary or coercive bringing together of people or people and objects," which "involves the pushing of another in a specific direction or toward a specific destination" (72). Finally, recognizing provides "the referencing submechanism of linking," establishing the relevance of "bridging, buffering, blocking out and channeling activities" (73). It includes "the labeling of people, things and events as good or bad, right or wrong, better or worse" (73), and thus as desirable or undesirable for inclusion.

In my childhood and adolescence, mealtime served an important bridging function: the family always ate together, and an essential feature of every meal was the reading of the Bible and prayer (grace before the meal, thanks after the meal). Breakfast reading was from a children's Bible (DeVries 1961), and I grew to love these stories as much as my favorite Christian fiction, also read to us regularly by our parents (Vandehulst 1963).

During Sunday morning worship services there was a strong emphasis on linking, entire families sitting together. My father took great pride on those occasions when all his offspring (three sons and seven daughters) could be together at church, filling an entire row on both sides of the aisle (ironically the aisle seats all bore the initials *PT*, indicating their previous presence in the local theater and documenting that the line between sacred and secular may be arbitrary indeed!). Buffering was accomplished by attending after-church Sunday school classes defined by grade level and by permitting the children to sit with their friends for the evening services; the adolescent boys who served as ushers traditionally sat together at the back of the church for both services, one of the fringe benefits that ensured no shortage of volunteers. Connections with the rest of the church community were also part of the Sunday tradition: children routinely spent the day (for dinner, an afternoon of play, and supper) with another family, and entire families visited each other's homes for coffee and dessert after the evening service, offering the opportunity for adult conversation, children's play, and occasional communal singing. Singing together, around the piano or organ, was a favorite pastime for the Vande Kemps. When my father was hospitalized with leukemia one Christmas Eve, we donned our fanciest dress and gathered in his room to sing traditional carols in both English and Dutch, a gift that moved him deeply and also serves as one of my cherished memories. When we held a family reunion at a Christian campground in the late 1970s, it was our sibling group (and in-laws) that provided most of the volunteer choir and the organist for Sunday morning outdoor worship, transforming a family hobby into an offering.

Blocking out occurred most overtly in the context of participation in the Lord's Supper, which was limited to those adolescents and adults who had publicly professed their faith. This was linked to a wider bounding mechanism: in the Christian Reformed Church, those who were not members of a specific congregation could not partake of the sacrament without prior permission of the consistory, the ruling body of the congregation. The strongest form of blocking out is embodied in the doctrine of double predestination as articulated in the Westminster Confession of 1647: "By the decree of God, for the manifestation of his glory, some men and angels are predestinated unto everlasting life, and others foreordained to everlasting death" (Office of the General Assembly 1983, 6.016). This is a succinct summary of the more extensive discussion in the Canons of Dort (1618–19), in which the first major point of doctrinal dispute concerns divine election and reprobation (see *Ecumenical Creeds* 1987, art. 1–18). The church fathers at Dordrecht taught that God's grace elected some to salvation, just as God's justice relegated others to reprobation. One of my sisters recently experienced an episode of suicidal depression (probably a menopausal psychosis) marked by the conviction that she was chosen for damnation, and this conviction has led her to resign church membership, since no amount of piety could now affect her destiny. It is interesting that she too appears to distinguish faith from theology (and polity), as she continues to pray and set aside time to "be with God." The double-predestination doctrine often leads the self-proclaimed elect to either complacency or arrogance and the damned to an excruciating form of abandonment anxiety. It leaves the unassured believer in a considerable quandary, since the Belgic Confession (first penned in 1561) also indicates that "all who withdraw from the church or do not join it act contrary to God's ordinance" (*Ecumenical Creeds* 1987, art. 28), and the Canons of Dort themselves include the admonition that those who have not yet experienced God's grace "ought not to be alarmed at the mention of reprobation, nor to count themselves among the reprobate" (art. 16). The theologically informed know, of course, that huge "cans of worms" are opened by this example—I myself have spent hours trying to think of a simple statement that would put it in theological perspective. For the family therapist there is a simpler message: one's early experience or identity is not formed only in the family. From the beginning, children in families like mine hear statements about belongingness and separateness that have far greater ramifications than do the family boundaries. The family itself derives its identity from a religious perspective that defines larger systems to which family members belong and to which they owe their loyalty.

Regular attendance at church, catechism class, and Sunday school obviously required some channeling, especially during the critical period of adolescence. Our family was a fairly closed one in this respect: church attendance was not negotiable, except during those years when small children required a Sunday night baby-sitter, a role for which we of course eagerly volunteered. Memory tells me it was different in the Netherlands, where small children were not expected to go to church and Sunday mornings included walks in the park with Dad while Mom and the others were in church. Christmas services, which small children did attend, were moments of genuine awe and worship, and I continue to cherish the Dutch carols heard on those occasions. Yet I connect the church services of my later childhood with two vivid and pleasant memories involving my mother: the taste of the King peppermints she routinely distributed at the beginning of the sermon and the scent of Boldoot cologne on her handkerchief—personal touches that engaged all the senses in worship and provided nurturance. Even now the taste and aroma are transitional objects, vivid reminders of the ambience of worship and of my ethnic heritage (for an excellent discussion of ethnicity and the family, see Ho 1987; McGoldrick, Pearce, and Giordano 1982).

Centering. Centering "consists of the developing, maintaining and transmitting of spatial guidelines for how traffic should flow within and across [the family's] borders" (Kantor and Lehr [1975] 1976, 74). These guidelines provide "the basis on which members form a coherent view of themselves and of the family, and so determine what they and it stand for" (74). Its subfunctions are *locating, gathering, designing, arranging,* and *spreading.* Locating, the referencing submechanism for centering, must identify the functional and dysfunctional elements of family life and search for elements which might enrich the family's identity. Gathering brings "people together to locate and identify what is right and wrong with their systems" (75). It may maintain the design of the system or challenge and question it. The mechanism of designing "gives birth to the articulated and unarticulated purposes of the family . . . [it] is the formulation of a general style in which the family desires to live" (75–76). The mechanism of arranging works out "an accommodation between the design the family has developed for itself and the situation in which it finds itself" (76). Finally, spreading disseminates "the desired shape of a family to all its members" and is "accompanied by certain key meanings, often credos or central family beliefs" (77).

Our centering was primarily covert. Guidelines were derived from an interaction of religious values and an extended family tradition. As a young child I was aware of, but did not participate in, conferences involving my parents and older siblings in which they resolved conflicts between secular and religious values. For example, rather than allow us to attend the Lenten Carnival (with its overtones of both Catholicism and immorality), my parents and older siblings planned special treats for the entire family. Since Carnival was a major celebration for the Dutch Catholics, my parents were sensitive to the feelings their teenagers might have if they were left out of the celebrations enjoyed by their peers (see "Carnival" 1941; "Carnival" 1951; for a delightful description of a Carnival celebration in the Dutch colonies, see Davey 1982). Such conferences did not occur during my adolescence, and I sensed that my parents acquiesced to the standards articulated by the "elders" of the church we attended, a group which in later years included my father—his common sense was much valued in this role, and at his death the minister was one of his chief mourners. Yet there is no doubt that our centering was contaminated by our painful assimilation into the American church and its surrounding culture, which apparently overwhelmed my parents.

The family in the Netherlands had been designed in a context that included an impressive network of extended family (Dad was 1 of 12 children; Mom, 1 of 4), which provided friendships as well as established a social calendar (for the celebration of birthdays, wedding anniversaries, and so on). We lived in a small Dutch town, which both provided and established ready access to neighbors. We traveled by bus and bicycle or on foot. Automobile trips were rare, since we owned no car, and we relied on geographically distant relatives to come to us; all of us relied on other forms of transportation. Rural Michigan was a drastic change indeed, and there were few substitutes for our relatives and close neighbors. My parents suddenly had to rely on acquaintanceships and relationships with coworkers. Traffic to the outside was necessary, and most of us established new relationships quickly, but not the true friendships that encouraged traffic *into* the family. Good friends were always welcome—we were encouraged to bring them home, and those visits often lasted overnight or for an entire week—but these did not come from the local church. And yet we really had nowhere else to turn, and a new identity emerged only as various family members formed relationships elsewhere and when my parents formed a friendship with the new pastor and his wife, a couple who understood my parents' past identity and helped to connect past and present frames of reference. Thus, in our case the local church hindered our centering rather than facilitated it. I think we all knew it was a bad environment for us, but the rules made it too costly to "leave the field" by joining another denomination or to drive farther to a more congenial congregation. In fact, we stayed where we were even when a new congregation was established locally—an act of loyalty that sacrificed family welfare to church politics at various levels of the denominational hierarchy. (On family dynamics in the church, see the chapter by Hibbs in this volume.)

Time

The family's relationship to time can be measured by both clock and calendar. Days and weeks are divided into "work times and play times, busy times and leisure times" (Kantor and Lehr [1975] 1976, 43) which provide cycles and rhythms for "the family dance," in which members may be "in phase" or "out of phase" with each other (79). Its subfunctions are *orienting, clocking,* and *synchronizing.*

Orienting. Orienting refers to "the selecting, directing, and maintaining of attitudes and behavior toward the past, present, future, and non-temporal realms of experience by emphasizing one or more of these realms or of the particular relationship among them" (Kantor and Lehr [1975] 1976, 78–79). Past orienting is characterized by "a remembering, re-experiencing, or re-enacting of something that has already taken place or existed" with the goal of retrieving or holding onto history, both intra- and extrafamilial (79). Present orienting emphasizes the spontaneous and may exclude "both tradition and vision" (80). Future orienting emphasizes "what is to come by anticipating, imagining, and/or planning for it" (80) and provides the family with a sense of vision, realistic or not. Nontemporal orienting consists of "events unrelated to calendar time," such as "fantasizing, dreaming, meditating, in private time unbound by past, present, or future calendar time constraints" (81). It is the realm of creativity and invention, hallucination and illusion.
    Christian theology implicitly integrates past, present, and future for its adherents. God's existence itself transcends time,

as summarized in the familiar words of Revelation 1:8 AB: "I am the Alpha and the Omega, *the Beginning and the End*, says the Lord God, He Who is and Who was and Who is to come, the Almighty (the Ruler of all)." Christians remember, re-experience, and re-enact various incidents in biblical and church history. Remembrance is explicit in the fourth of the Ten Commandments: "Remember the sabbath day, to keep it holy" (Exod. 20:8 RSV; for the significance of *remember*, see Office of the General Assembly 1983, 7.231). In the church of my youth, the Ten Commandments were read every Sunday. Many of them illustrate the interface of centering and orienting: we were reminded weekly of creation and redemption history to inspire lives of Christian gratitude. Remembrance became experiential in the Lord's Supper, a quarterly event in the church year. As described in the Second Helvetic Confession of 1566, the Lord's Supper is a "Memorial of God's Benefits" in which we commemorate the redeeming work of Christ (Office of the General Assembly 1983, 5.195). Here, we have an event which mingles time past (commemoration) with time present (participation and fellowship) and the nontemporal (bread and wine symbolize the body and blood of Christ, who is present spiritually rather than bodily). The present for the Christian is anchored in *anno Domini* (A.D.), "the year of our Lord," which roots the Gregorian calendar in *evangelium*, salvation history. Yet this recalls a Christ who in the present works for reconciliation in the church and expects such reconciliation from its members (see the Confession of 1967 in Office of the General Assembly 1983, 9.01, 9.25).

Christian life is also oriented toward the future. In the Nicene Creed of the fourth century, the believer asserts that the Lord Jesus Christ "shall come again with glory to judge both the quick and the dead, whose kingdom shall have no end" (Office of the General Assembly 1983, 1.2). The creed ends with the statement, "And we look for the resurrection of the dead, and the life of the world to come" (1.3). The more tersely worded Apostles' Creed (familiar to me from my childhood, when I recited it every Lord's Day) asserts that Christ shall come from "the right hand of God" to "judge the quick and the dead" and ends with "I believe in . . . the resurrection of the body; and the life everlasting" (2.2–2.3). Resurrection, judg-

ment, and eternal life/damnation are core furture-oriented constructs in Christian theology.

Clocking. Clocking regulates "the sequence, frequency,
duration, and pace of immediately experienced events from
moment to moment, hour to hour, and day to day" and "is concerned with the daily cycles of time, or with those cycles occur-
ring within a day" (Kantor and Lehr [1975] 1976, 82). Its subfunctions are *sequencing, frequency setting, duration setting,
pacing,* and *scheduling.* Sequencing is "employed by families to
develop and maintain an order to events." Family rules are
established "to help illuminate and stabilize certain priorities"
(83), which contribute to the family's uniqueness. Frequency
setting is concerned with "how often events are repeated," thus
developing and maintaining "patterns of repetition" (83), creating security as well as the possible extremes of boredom and
unpredictability. Duration setting is concerned with time limits
for family and individual activities. Pacing is the regulation of
both the absolute rate or speed of events and "the variations in
speed from one point in time to another" (84). The clocking functions are regulated by scheduling, which sets their "sequence,
frequency, duration, and/or pace" (85).

Sacred events comprised a highly reliable sequence in our
family's life. Scheduled prayer and Bible reading at mealtimes
and prayer at bedtime sanctified the hours of the day. Sunday
church services and midweek catechism classes punctuated the
week, with special rules observed on the Lord's Day. Thus,
sacred space penetrated secular space in a predictable sequence,
a process recognized and made explicit in Thomas Howard's
Hallowed Be This House:

> . . . we do, in fact, walk daily among the hallows; . . . we will have
> to recover the sense of the hallowed as being all around us. We
> will have to open our eyes and try to see once more the common-
> place as both blocking and revealing the holy to us. We will have
> to refuse resolutely the secularism that has made ordinariness
> unholy. . . .
>   I would like to suggest that at least one place (among others)
> which may be hallowed anew as the place where the celebration
> of all the mysteries may occur, and where all of life may be
> offered up in oblation to the Most High, is the family household.
> ([1976] 1979, 13–14)

The Heidelberg Catechism, with its 52 Lord's Days, ensured consecration of the entire year. Inevitably, such constant exposure led to a mastery of sacred facts and creeds: memorization of the Bible and the catechism were rituals for the acquisition of a Christian meaning system. Important days on the calendar included many associated with the liturgical year: Christmas, Palm Sunday, Good Friday, Easter, Ascension Day, Pentecost, Thanksgiving, and (in the Netherlands) Reformation Day. These sacred events required church attendance and featured elements of both commemoration and celebration.

Synchronizing. Synchronizing "is the temporal equivalent of the spatial mechanism, centering," and includes both "the creation and execution of temporal guidelines" (Kantor and Lehr [1975] 1976, 86). Its subfunctions are *monitoring, priority setting, coordinating, reminding,* and *programming.* Monitoring involves "the recurring assessment of whether the family's use of time is beneficial" and constitutes "the referencing submechanism of synchronizing" through which the family "assesses the degree of satisfaction it is experiencing as a consequence of the life it has been evolving" (86–87). Priority setting determines which events "are most important for family members" (87), thus linking the time and power dimensions and often generating conflict. Programming refers to "the developing of guidelines for how to use time in pursuit of a family life plan" and "produces a conception of who and what the family wants to become" (87). Coordinating is the function which explicitly or implicitly "organizes and adjusts [family] members' movements so that they are in some synchronization with each other, and in accord with the family program" (88). Finally, reminding is the function, often motivated by discontent, by which "families make their members aware of what their life plan program is, its origin, the way in which it is to be maintained and enforced, and how it can be altered" (88–89).

In our family, questions about allotment of time were related to both the sacred schedule and the realities of the blue-collar work world. Regular attendance at Sunday worship and Saturday morning or Wednesday evening catechism was nonnegotiable. Other church activities involved more conscious monitoring, priority setting, programming, coordinating, and reminding. Less frequent events, such as monthly meetings of the ladies' aid or the consistory, parties for the young people's group, choir rehearsal, or summer vacation Bible school might engender both discussion and negotiation, and it was acceptable to express frustration at the complexity of their scheduling. By the time I was of college age and working at a summer job, the local congregation had adapted to the increased employment of women (who were expected to do the teaching) by scheduling the vacation Bible school in the evening; it was taken for granted that we'd somehow find the energy for teaching despite having worked all day and working again the next. Reminders were of course needed for study of the catechism and Sunday-school papers, which was frequently less rewarding than other kinds of homework.

Family Development: A Short Digression

Religious practices and beliefs in my family were associated with every stage of individual and family development (for overviews of family development, see Carter and McGoldrick 1988; Falicov 1988; Pittman 1987). Christian faith relies on many Old Testament passages that speak of God's role in creation, conception, and pregnancy—the earliest stages in identity formation. The psalmist states:

> For you created my inmost being;
>   you knit me together in my mother's womb.
> I praise you because I am fearfully and wonderfully made;
>   your works are wonderful,
>   I know that full well.
> My frame was not hidden from you
>   when I was made in the secret place.
> When I was woven together in the depths of the earth,
>   your eyes saw my unformed body.
> All the days ordained for me
>   were written in your book
>   before one of them came to be.
>
> [Ps. 139:13–16 NIV]

A beautiful contemporary statement of this is made in D. Ivan Dykstra's essay "Who Am I?":

> Identity is . . . a matter of theology.
> It's what you *are*, beyond the ravages of time.

> And that can only be that in the sight of God,
>   in some 10 million million years there'll never
>   be another you.
> He knows you, and He knows you by your name.
> In every other sense you're finally replaceable,
>   repeatable, forgettable, and losable.
> . . . you start with that.
> Some things must be at the beginning or they'll
>   never be.
> We do not search for that; we start from that. (1983, 6–7)

Following birth, the sacrament of baptism (or a service of dedication) provides identity for the infant and stresses its belongingness in the community. Thus, the Presbyterian "Directory for the Service of God," which is typical of Reformed liturgy, asserts that

> Christian parents have the right to present their infant children for baptism as a sign and seal of God's promise to them as heirs of the covenant. In presenting a child for baptism parents affirm in public their duty to bring up the child to love and serve God. The congregation, too, promises to surround the child with their love and concern in Christ, that the child may continue in the community of the church, confess Jesus Christ as Savior and Lord, and live in God's eternal Kingdom. (Office of the General Assembly 1986–87, S–3.0300)

The baptism or dedication of a child is an occasion for celebration in the Christian family and church, an occasion to invite the participation of the extended family. It connects the newborn child with the history of the church and previous generations of the family, extending the circle of belongingness and strengthening the core of identity.

In our family the christening gown was a family heirloom that made the baptism a "linking" event. In line with the baptismal vows, considerable attention was paid to the Christian education of the children, which included an informal education achieved through Bible stories and Christian literature and a formal education achieved through Sunday school, vacation Bible school, and catechism with their prepared curricula and through Christian schooling (often an expense leading to considerable sacrifice). My first two school years in the Netherlands were spent in the Christian school where my siblings had gone

before me. There we learned in more detail the stories of the
Bible and significant episodes in church history (and were sub-
jected to discipline matching that of boot camp). I have poignant
memories of being curled up in bed next to my brother, my sister on his other side, as he described in detail the Children's
Crusades, which he was studying in school—I remember only
the nurture of his storytelling; my sister recalls primarily the
horror of these historical events which represent the shadow
side of Christianity. In adolescence, we faced the important public confession of faith, the transition ritual into adulthood both
at church and at home: a child who could make such a significant commitment could also be trusted with other major decisions. Yet I found that my parents were displeased when I
selected a college sponsored by the Reformed Church in
America (RCA) rather than one of our own denomination. This
was, I think, less connected with particular religious beliefs
(since the doctrinal differences between the CRC and the RCA
are minor) than with strong European ideas about social class
and hierarchy: our kind of people (especially the girls) did not
go to college, and if we did, we should defer to authorities in the
selection process. I, however, resorted to my ethnic and family
heritage of stubbornness and remained firm in my choice: I felt
I was entitled to choose how I should spend my own money, and
I needed to pursue the possibility of a subculture that was more
affirming. Having played by the rules my entire adolescence, I
collapsed all my rebellion into that one act of defiance, knowing
that it was somehow essential to my survival. Perhaps I also
knew, even then, that the politics of our denomination were not
crucial to the family's meaning system and that my choice was
true to what we were at the core.

In the Christian theology of marriage we see reflected the
relational nature of Christian theology (Vande Kemp and
Schreck 1981; also see Schreck's contribution to this volume:
chap. 3, "Personhood and Relational Life Tasks"). The Second
Helvetic Confession addresses itself to those who have the "gift
of celibacy," implying that few will have this calling and that
most will opt for marriage, which "was instituted by the Lord
God himself" (Office of the General Assembly 1983, 5.246). It
also affirms the civil laws against incest, advises that marriage
not be pursued without parental consent (5.247), and provides
for matrimonial courts (5.248). The Westminster Confession

reflects additional concerns about polygamy, divorce and remarriage, adultery, and the importance of selecting a Christian partner (Office of the General Assembly 1983, 6.131–39). Thus, the Reformed understanding of marriage recognizes the need for belonging, rejects the enmeshment associated with incest, and affirms the separation of Christians from non-Christians (another form of blocking out). Since the latter included Catholics, one older sister of mine married her Catholic husband only after my mother's death and converted to Catholicism only after my father's—decisions which reflected her desire not to inflict unnecessary pain on our parents. The experience has taught her that the subcultural differences connected with Catholicism and Protestantism require considerable negotiation in life's daily decision making, as is discussed by Barbara D. Schiappa (1982).

The Confession of 1967, the most recent, affirms interracial marriage (Office of the General Assembly 1983, 9.44) and challenges Christians to marital responsibility and commitment (9.47), rejecting the sexual anarchy of the 1960s for a return to the basic value of chastity (4.108–9). Although the attainment of the ideal is more often a goal than a reality, marriages guided by this meaning system benefit from renewed efforts to work through conflict and the recognition that it is God's help rather than their unstable love that will see them through difficult times. The commitment goes beyond their relationship to include the church and God. Thus, both in marriage and divorce Christian couples rightly ask, "What will people think?" as their marital vows are given in a public worship service that defines marriage as a covenant as well as a contract and the wedding reception as a celebration of Christian community as well as personal and familial joy. The covenant of marriage is one rich in metaphorical and historical significance. So binding was the marital contract in biblical Judaism, and so salient the notion of marital intimacy and love, that Christ spoke of himself as the bridegroom and later writers speak of the New Testament church as the bride of Christ. Thus, the relationship between husband and wife is informed by, and in turn affects the interpretation of, the relationship between Christ and the church. It is this connection that so powerfully links the idea of divorce with alienation from God. In fact, the church fears that permitting divorce will weaken the meaning of Christ's relationship to us, a misunderstanding (and form of eisegesis) that occurs even among highly educated theologians and illustrates our powerful dependence on metaphors and the resistance of systematic theology to the natural emergence of new symbols which carry meaning and transform traditional categories.

In the Christian world view, death is an inevitable result of the fallen human condition. It is appropriately associated with the grief of separation and loss, but also marks the end of sin and misery, brings us into the presence of God, and signals the hope of the resurrection. The occasion of death provides opportunity for the exercise of Christian community and support and the experience of God's comfort to the bereaved. What is uniquely Reformed about a funeral or memorial service lies in what the Presbyterian church now calls the "Service of Witness to the Resurrection" (Office of the General Assembly 1986–87, S5.0500), which requires that even in our grief we glorify God and commemorate Christ's victory over death. This perspective is reflected in several requiem masses that depart from the classic Catholic mass for the dead by omitting the "day of wrath" (*dies irae*), which features so dominantly, for example, in Giuseppe Verdi's magnificent *Messa da Requiem* and which is the "most dramatic sequence" in that text (Goodwin 1987, 16). Instead, these masses focus on the comfort of the resurrection. Thus, Johannes Brahms's much-loved *German Requiem* "addresses those who mourn, offering them consolation. . . . Death is regarded only from the viewpoint of the sorrow experienced by the bereaved, with the final resurrection and judgment referred to only as a promise for the future" (Kross n.d.). The exquisite Gabriel Fauré *Requiem* similarly focuses on paradise. Fauré himself defended this focus: "It has been said that my *Requiem* does not express the fear of death, and it has been called a lullaby of death. But it is thus that I see death: as a happy deliverance, an inspiration towards happiness above, rather than a painful experience" (cited by Barker [1988], who regards the Fauré *Requiem* as "the very opposite of Verdi's"). Thus, the Reformed approach to death shrouds it with meaning and emphasizes future time and the nontemporal, linking human and divine time in that realm where "one day is as a thousand years, and a thousand years as one day" (2 Pet. 3:8 RSV).

Energy

The energy dimension refers to the ways in which families charge and discharge energy operations. Charging refers to "the accumulation of energy," and discharging refers to "the expending of it" (Kantor and Lehr [1975] 1976, 44). The family's successful functioning depends on a "nearly even ratio of charge to discharge in the course of time" (44). In assessing the family's energy-related functions, we must ask several questions:

> Does the family expend enough energy to meet the demands placed on it? Does it overextend itself, undertaking more demands and expending more energy than it can hope to supply? Do legitimate energy demands go unmet? Do members have satisfying outlets for their energies? Are family energies squandered? (45)

The energy functions are *fueling, investing,* and *mobilizing,* each of which includes several subfunctions.

Fueling. Fueling regulates the acquisition of energy, which is primarily an individual, private event. However, its mode must be approved by other family members, and this is responsible for many family conflicts. The fueling subfunctions are *surveying, tapping, charging, storing,* and *requisitioning.* The individual must survey the environment in order to locate sources of energy which may potentially be tapped. Kantor and Lehr indicate that "many critical family battles are fought over how or in what ways fueling is to take place, especially over what sources members may tap and what sources they may not. . . . What sources members tap often turns into a discussion of both individual and group morality" ([1975] 1976, 93). Charging takes place when energy is actually taken in, and it is essential for family growth and development. Energy is stored when the family develops and maintains "a reservoir of available energy in the forms of meanings, images, feelings, and/or body responses" (94). Negative or positive energy is stored in all remembered items. Requisitioning is the referencing mechanism for fueling that permits family members to "comment about their fueling processes" (95).

Investing. Investing refers to "the regulation of expending or discharging energies to targets and bearers of targets" (Kantor and Lehr [1975] 1976, 95). Its subfunctions are *reconnoitering, attaching, committing, detaching,* and *accounting.* Reconnoitering locates and selects "targets for family energies" (95), which become foci for attaching operations. Such operations are "a fertile ground for family conflict. Which ideas, beliefs, people or causes one ought to choose as targets for one's energy inevitably produces differing opinions and conflicting actions" (97). Committing involves the "devotion of energies to targets. . . . Serious difficulties develop whenever members are required to commit more energy to a target than they wish or are able to devote, or when they are not permitted by family regulation to commit the amount of energies they wish to" (97). Commitments of negative energy destroy targets. Detaching involves the disconnection or removal of energy. Unwanted detachments may be experienced as "intense emotional deprivation" (98). Arbitrary and nonnegotiable detachments may lead individuals to "feel irrationally regulated and robbed" (98). Complete and universal detachment constitutes "an emotional withdrawal from all social interaction" (98). Investments are monitored through the accounting function, which tracks energy commitments and determines whether they are sufficient and beneficial. Accounting provides both a checkpoint and a safety valve for investment strategies.

Mobilizing. The mobilizing mechanism is used to "develop and implement guidelines for regulating the total flow of energy" (Kantor and Lehr [1975] 1976, 98) and establishes the energy rhythm. Its subfunctions are *gauging, budgeting, mustering, transforming,* and *distributing.* Gauging, the reference function, takes "an inventory to determine how much energy is needed" (99), using signals such as fatigue and apathy. Budgeting reflects the family's "plan for regulating the flow of [its] energy" (100). Mustering is the function which rouses and focuses energy. Mustering crises occur with energy deficits and energy diffusion. Transforming is the function families use to regulate the level, form, and charge of their energies. Finally, distributing involves the "assigning and conducting of energy from where it is available to where it is needed, or attracted" (101).

Faith has, through the ages, proved itself a reliable energy source: church attendance and other religious activities all potentially energize. Whether it is through the solitude of prayer, the fellowship of other Christians, the comfort of the liturgy and ritual, the wonder of grace and forgiveness, the inspiration of music, the achievement of mastery (having learned one's creeds or portions of Scripture), fascination with biblical stories, the promises of the future, the exhortation of a sermon, the deep spiritual involvement of the sacraments, or a sermon that speaks to one's deepest pain, Christian worship energizes. As a child I looked forward to these various religious activities because they offered an opportunity to see friends and to play. I loved the music, and I often received affirmation through mastery. As an adolescent, elements of friendship continued to energize me, but I also found great meaning in the gospel itself, which provided a strong sense of identity and a basis for peer relationships. Today I continue to draw nourishment from the hearing of the Word of God, participation in Holy Communion, the community of other Christians, the layers of truth revealed in religious fiction, and the majesty of classical sacred music. These sources of energy are rooted in both family and church life.

Energy investments in the sacred sphere often overlap with energy sources, and the creeds also assist in the selection of targets for family energies. The Larger Catechism commences with a purpose statement that guides all energy investments:

Q. 1. What is the chief and highest end of [humankind]?
A. [Our] chief and highest end is to glorify God, and fully to enjoy [God] forever. (Office of the General Assembly 1983, 7.111)

Further direction on this issue comes from the various guides to Christian worship. For example, in the Presbyterian *Book of Order* there are guidelines for stewardship of both time and resources:

The Holy Scripture teaches that God is the owner of all persons and all things, and that people are but stewards of life and possessions; that God's ownership and their stewardship should be acknowledged; that this acknowledgement should take the form, in part, of giving a worthy proportion of their income to the church of Jesus Christ, of giving themselves in dedication to

God, of giving service to others in God's behalf, thus worshiping the Lord with all they have and are. Furthermore, all not given more directly to God should be used as a Christian testimony to God and to the world. (Office of the General Assembly 1986–87, S–2.0900)

In our family, church-related activities were, with little exception, accepted as legitimate uses of one's time and energy, as long as they did not interfere with one's work or require an additional financial investment. We were a large, low-income family, and it was sometimes a hardship that our denomination operated with a per-family financial quota system which was enforced literally by our particular congregation, a custom not practiced by the churches in which I have been an officer as an adult. My father's blue-collar jobs also made it difficult for him to participate in higher-level church government in the way I participate now: assembly lines do not run well when even one worker leaves before the shift is completed, nor could the family's income have done without those hours on the job.

On at least one occasion in our family's life, we suffered from a misdirection of religious energy, which was manifested in serious religious pathology. One sister, who probably played the role of the family scapegoat—a powerful religious symbol family theorists borrowed from Judaism—developed severe obsessive-compulsive symptoms that included long hours of prayer and Bible reading, extensive cleansing rituals, suicidal gestures, and anorexia. This was in the early 1960s, before the advent of the family therapy revolution, and her hospitalization was followed by foster care rather than family treatment. This event depleted the family's resources financially and emotionally and created the only occasion in my memory involving a serious upheaval in the family structure. The usual structure was characterized by a strong hierarchy (consistent with a Calvinistic world view) that entailed a clear parental role and the division of the sibling subsystem into "the big kids" and "the little kids." Because my parents were ill-equipped to deal with mental illness, they relied on the "expertise" of my older sisters who were trained at Pine Rest, a Christian psychiatric hospital sponsored by several Reformed denominations. It was a source of acute shame to everyone that our faith needed supplementing in this way. My personal response was a questioning that led me beyond the boundaries of faith into the realm of family theory to understand the dynamics underlying my sister's pathological use of religious ritual and my own nascent symptoms during the short period she spent at home before going to foster care—sure evidence that the family at that time needed to be restructured in some way.

Family Types

Kantor and Lehr define three "family types which are based on three different homeostatic models" ([1975] 1976, 116):

In the closed family system, stable structures (fixed space, regular time, and steady energy) are relied upon as reference points for order and change. In the open family system, order and change are expected to result from the interaction of relatively stable evolving family structures (movable space, variable time, and flexible energy). In the random system, unstable structures (dispersed space, irregular time, and fluctuating energy) are experimented with as reference points for order and change. (119)

Kantor and Lehr's discussion of the target dimensions is structured around these three types of families. Thus, the authors state that "stability within and across all six dimensions of family process is the core purpose of the closed-type family. . . . The purpose of [the] open-style process is to create a system that is adaptive to the needs of both individual and family systems. . . . [and] the core purpose of random family system process can best be summed up as free exploration" (144).

Target Dimensions

Kantor and Lehr ([1975] 1976) identified three target dimensions which define the goals of family process. They "think of the interior social space of the family as an enclosure such as a sphere or a cube. Within this three-dimensional physical analogue, most, if not all, of a family's substantive transactions take place" (Kantor and Lehr [1975] 1976, 46). Within this metaphor, they "conceive of affect events as lateral relations, power events as vertical relations, and meaning events as depth relations" (46), so that distance regulation becomes a process of regulating events along these three axes.

Affect

The affect dimension encompasses "sentient experiences and moral expressions . . . that are evaluated and experienced along a continuum of the positive and the negative" (Kantor and Lehr [1975] 1976, 46). In family life, the primary affective targets are "affirmative intimacy and nurturance" (46): "We define intimacy as a condition of mutual emotional closeness, often intense closeness, among peers. Nurturance is an exchange in which one or more family members receive emotional support and encouragement from another member or members. Thus, whereas intimacy involves a two-directional emotional exchange, nurturance implies a primarily undirectional flow of affect" (47).

Affect also refers to such issues as "affiliation, loyalty, emotional acceptance, and affirmation" (Kantor and Lehr [1975] 1976, 47). Within the affect arena, family members are constantly learning and relearning "how and when joinings and separations are tolerable, optimal, or intolerable" (47); at the extremes, they experience fusion or alienation. The types of families differ in their affect ideals: "Durability, fidelity and sincerity are the closed systems' ideals in the affect dimension. . . . responsiveness, authenticity, and the legitimacy of emotional latitude are the open systems' major affect ideals" (145). Ecstasy, "whimsicality and spontaneity" are the affect ideals for the random system (146).

Affect dimensions are included in much of Christian theology and provide the context for Christian rules of conduct. The Christian church stresses the dynamics of forgiveness, grace, gratitude, loyalty, and community (Hiltner 1972). Christ, when asked which of the Ten Commandments was the greatest, answered: "You shall love the Lord your God with all your heart, and with all your soul, and with all your mind. This is the great and first commandment. And a second is like it, You shall love your neighbor as yourself" (Matt. 22:37–39 RSV). In the Reformed interpretation, the Ten Commandments are guides for a life of gratitude—thus, the Heidelberg Catechism includes them not in the section on sin, but in its later discussion of the sanctified life. The Christian definition of community, based on Christ's commandment of love, leans heavily on metaphors derived from family life: we are to be brothers and sisters in Christ, thus, to treat all believers as kin.

These principles of conduct shaped much of what is distinctive in my life. I have often been told that I am generous because of actions performed instinctively in response to an implicit assumption that "the fellowship of saints" can thrive only through nonpossessive mutuality. When I pay the monthly bills, the check to the church precedes all the others, an action growing out of the conviction that if we provide for the work of the church, God will provide for our needs. This provision for the needy has from the inception of the church been the function of deacons and characterizes all the church bodies of my recent acquaintance, which give generously to feed and shelter the homeless locally and to provide assistance to famine-ravished and impoverished Third-World countries and other areas suffering from the impact of natural disasters such as earthquakes, floods, and hurricanes. Unfortunately, my poverty-level parents had a great fear of charity, which they passed to their children. Several siblings were embarrassed when my youngest sister and her husband accepted a mission assignment for which they "raised their support," an act regarded as a form of begging. And when my oldest sister was a young widowed mother, it was difficult for her to accept that she was among those to whom the deacons were called to minister. The lesson of receiving graciously is generally not learned as easily as that of giving graciously, and it is one with which I struggled for many years (for a theoretical discussion of this issue, which integrates Christian theology and contextual family theory, see Vande Kemp 1987).

The affect dimension in our family and local congregation was no doubt heavily influenced by our ethnic heritage: the Dutch are not a race famous for their emotional expression. What Hinda Winawer-Steiner and Norbert A. Wetzel say of German families applies to the Dutch as well: "People seem to contain what they might experience as too explosive through boundaries, structure, and emotional control" (1982, 255). These authors speak of the German tradition of *Gemütlichkeit*, "the experience of familiarity, emotional closeness, and fun . . . the capacity to share warmth and conviviality" (255). The

Dutch use the related *gezelligheit*, a term my sibs and I might use to describe the following family experiences: walking with Mom on a Sunday afternoon to the woods and the huge boulder that lay there (we have a photograph from one such occasion, and the smiles on all the faces reveal our sheer delight); playing a game of Monopoly or Scrabble with Dad on a Sunday afternoon; gathering around the piano or organ for a songfest on a Sunday afternoon or evening; celebrating privately on New Year's Eve; drinking coffee around the kitchen table on a Saturday evening or Fizzies on the porch on Sunday afternoon, after Mom woke from her nap; gathering (the sisters and Mom) in the kitchen to wash the dishes after enjoying Sunday dinner. Intimacy was present, but it was characterized by "comfort in the presence of the other" rather than emotional vulnerability. The same comfortableness mixed with fun was present at local church functions such as weddings, with their informal church-basement receptions to which everyone was invited, and the annual potluck Sunday school picnic—traditions which were part of our religious reference group.

Power

Kantor and Lehr define power as "the freedom to decide what we want, and the ability to get it" ([1975] 1976, 37). This is a definition of "constructive efficacy" (49), and it alludes to "matters of individual, conceptual, and intersocial volition" (48). Power implies verticality, which in turn is "associated with issues of dominance, submission, and mediation, hindrance and furtherance, opposition and cooperation, competition and association, option and necessity, and superiority and inferiority" (48). A family's "power relations determine who and what will move freely, and who and what will be restrained" (49) and affect one's "status in the family hierarchy, decision making, concepts of property, [and] of rights and responsibilities" (49). Extremes on this dimension are identified with tyranny and anarchy.

Again, the three family types differ in their orientation to power. The closed system strives for *stable* efficacy through "authority, discipline, and preparation" (Kantor and Lehr [1975] 1976, 146). Competence is an assumption paired with the expectation that one will strive for perfection, which is best attained by apprenticeship to "something bigger than the self" (146) and allegiance to the law. The system rule is "persevere and you shall prevail" (146). Its typical member "chooses to observe and conform and in so doing acquires his [or her] autonomy from above" (146). The open family strives for *adaptive* efficacy through persuasion, negotiation, and a "decision-making dialectic" with synthesis, cooperation, and allowance as goals. Faith in the "basic goodness and wisdom of its members" (146) is the basic assumption that eventuates in its mandate "Persuade rather than coerce" (147). Autonomy and self-mastery are highly valued, but balanced with respect for others. Opposition is part of the resolution process and is valued because it respects individuation. The random system strives for *exploratory* efficacy which leads to the mandate "Discover your potential" (147). This system values free choice, experimentation, and challenge. Charisma is necessary in order to inspire others to follow one's direction, as coercion is unacceptable. Opposition can remain unresolved, as the system thrives on creative anarchy and "multiformity of purpose" (147). Ultimately, the role of power in the family underlines the interdependence of family members: they have the power to impede or facilitate each other's goals, power which may be most influential in the effort to attain one's goals of intimacy, nurturance, and competence.

Several years ago, as a participant in a symposium on power at Fuller Theological Seminary, I was asked to represent the family therapy perspective. I defined power with its interpersonal meaning as "the ability to get what you want." I was severely chastised by a member of the audience who accused me of putting my will before God's will, thus assuming an implicit conflict between my will and God's, an assumption not uncommon in Calvinist circles. While I successfully disqualified her accusation—I do try to follow the closed system's mandate of aligning myself with a higher power, in the person of God (and it was not her role to judge, in any case)—it is much more difficult to avoid the classic problem of freedom and determinism, which arose primarily because Christian theology posits an omniscient, omnipotent, and beneficent God and at the same time holds humankind responsible for its decisions. I often feel double-bound by this theology, but have been no more successful than Job at "leaving the field." However, it has perhaps been even more painful to confront the interpersonal version of this, which reflects the Calvinist preoccupation with depravity: I can recall numerous instances of being blamed for interpersonal problems and failures that I did not and could not have created, with no one's having the wisdom to tell me that in a relational world others often have the power to grant or refuse our wishes and dreams and to define the nature of our relationship. Apparently it was much easier to assume that I, personally, had sinned than that I was the victim of someone else's fallen condition. Calvinist theology reinforces childlike belief in one's own efficacy, so that the illusion of omnipotence is not extinguished. But it tends to be a one-sided omnipotence which blames the self for bad things that happen and gives God credit for the good, a situation that frequently leads to self-blame, depression, and fear.

It should be no surprise that Christians, like other mortals, hold ambivalent attitudes toward authority, power, and responsibility. Paul W. Pruyser (1968), in his perceptive discussion, notes that each of these is generally vested in organizations, including the family and the church; in thought structures and ideas, and thus in theological creeds and confessions; and in cultures, of which the church is a major repository. Churches manifest their approach to power and authority in their polity, or rules of organizational structure. Persons raised in Christian families often reflect complex attitudes that combine the family's particular approach to power with the polity of their religious denomination. The latter ranges from the hierarchical, patriarchal structure of Roman Catholicism to the aristocratic structure of Anglicanism, from the republican structure of the Reformed tradition to the democratic structure of Congregationalism. Pruyser astutely notes that polity is often as serious a consideration as theology, a dynamic which may explain the continued resistance of many denominations to the ordination of women to offices in the church: even the most democratic church polities have traditionally accorded power only to men, and generally it is those in power who have taken polity most seriously. As Pruyser remarks, this power holds only for those who choose to "play the game" by retaining their ties with a particular religious group.

I initially left the Christian Reformed denomination merely for geographic reasons; I later cut myself off from it by default, in accepting ordination as a ruling elder in a different denomination. The CRC, which in 1990 approved the ordination of women on a provisional basis, may ultimately split over this issue; my family has seldom questioned the patriarchal values, and most would probably defend them. Thus, the church becomes a source of both sex-role conflict and sex-role strain (see Hafner 1986) for literally thousands of women as they struggle to attain roles not approved of by their parents, siblings, spouses, children, and church authorities. These women are no longer able to believe the version of reality imposed by their religious leaders because they have felt too urgently God's sense of call, and are thus forced to engage in acts which are at worst interpreted as heretical and at best as disloyal (for further discussion of the role of loyalty in intergenerational family theory, see chap. 4 by Hibbs and chap. 5 by Krasner and Joyce in this volume).

Another manifestation of power in the church, in part related to church polity, is the layperson's attitude toward the clergy. Although I was raised in a denomination with a republican polity, our family (and the Dutch culture in which it was embedded) ascribed great authority to the minister. This in part reflected the cultural attitude of a lower-class family in a highly class-conscious European society, but it was packaged in a theology that regarded the minister as endowed with special virtues because of his religious calling. Perhaps this notion grew out of the embroidery of a child's mind as I was enjoined to obedience and submission, but to me the message was very clear that as laypeople we were inferior to the minister. The Reformed churches learned the dangers of this attitude—along with its admonitions concerning our obedience to the civil authorities (see, for example, art. 36 of the Belgic Confession)—during the Nazi persecution, which led to the 1934 Theological Declaration of Barmen (Office of the General Assembly 1983, 8.01–28), a "confession" actively rejecting the action of both secular and religious authorities (see Rogers 1985). Both the Barmen declaration and the Confession of 1967 (which focused especially on racism) accentuated a tension between those clergy who focused on the priestly functions of worship and pastoral care and those who emphasized the prophetic functions of "intellectual honesty and societal relevance" (Pruyser 1968, 266).

Like the institutional church, I have personally wrestled to integrate my understanding of Christian love and acceptance with the identity-maintaining differentiation between Christians and non-Christians. As a young adult I was thoroughly confused by my parents' failure to integrate their history with their theology: the latter reflected a theological anti-Semitism rooted in the belief that the Jews rejected the Messiah; the former included active involvement in the Dutch resistance to the German occupation and participation in the Jewish underground. I eventually chose the former as the more salient message, forming deep friendships with Jewish colleagues in graduate school and sharing with them in the celebration of Passover: the Seder was for me a highly meaningful symbolic initiation of Holy Week, connecting the Old and New Testaments in a kinship defined by a common tradition and the memory of the Holocaust. In my recent travels to the Holy Land, this unity of traditions (amidst their great diversity) was again confirmed, along with the ties that bind us to Catholicism and a variety of Middle Eastern churches. Meaning systems vary greatly among the diverse religious groups that make Jerusalem their home, but all acknowledge God as the ultimate source of power.

Meaning

The meaning dimension "encompasses all those actions and transactions relating to ideas and the communication of ideas about the family and the various worlds (social, spiritual, conceptual, and material) to which it relates" (Kantor and Lehr [1975] 1976, 50). The depth regulations of meaning "refer to the [family's] maintenance of identity as a living entity by the transmission of ideas about itself ('us') and the world ('them'), and by the management of sameness and difference in the organization of its shared conceptual life" (50–51). The primary target is "purposeful identity," defined as "an integrated sense of direction and destination, an awareness of who one is and what one would like to become. It is the antithesis of uncertainty, confusion, and disorientation" (51). Within the province of meaning are included "ideas, credos, values, ideologies, world views, and a sense of good and bad and right and wrong" (51). The primary measurable aspect of meaning is the degree to which it is shared, or held in common. Rigidity on this dimension leads to conformity of absolute meaning, conceptual isolation, and intellectual irrelevance. The three family types differ in their meaning ideals: "The closed system's meaning mandate is to **be integrated.** Certainty, unity, and clarity are its ideals. . . . The open system's meaning mandate is to **be authentic.** Relevance, affinity, and tolerance are its ideals. . . . The random system's mandate is to **be creative.** Ambiguity, diversity, and originality are its ideals" (148–49).

Meaning for the Christian family is provided in both Scripture and the creeds and confessions of the church, and it often comes intertwined with authority. As Pruyser notes, "Biblical power and authority are . . . both intrinsic and extrinsic: they lie in the persuasion of the texts as well as the institutional tradition which copied, edited, codified, and disseminated them" (1968, 268). As my tradition was strong in authority, I tended to interpret the Bible literally and according to the theology embodied in the Heidelberg Catechism. My family experience, while it strongly encouraged reading, did not reinforce independent thinking: books were read, and respected, as unquestionable repositories of "truth" and "right." Permission for questioning was given to me by several wise professors in college and graduate school, but even now the effects of such conditioning linger as I continue to question my right to challenge not only the great thinkers of the church but also my professional colleagues.

Fantasy also did not receive much reinforcement in the rational context of Reformed theology, and only in recent years did I realize that even my favorite childhood fiction (Vandehulst 1963) was "realist" in its orientation—with the exception of my favorite story in the entire collection, "The Ugly Caterpillar." I did not realize that the nurture of my intuitive side was at stake until one of my sisters refused to let her children read Madeleine L'Engle's (1962, 1973, 1978) "science fiction" trilogy—a set I consider among the best Christian fiction—because "those things didn't really happen." As an adult, I have rejected this assumption that so clearly disqualified my experience and found understanding in a mind as great as that of C. S. Lewis, who asserts that "the story does what no theorem can quite do. It may not be 'like real life' in the superficial sense: but it sets before us an image of what reality may well be like at some more central region" ([1947] 1973, 101). I have learned the legitimacy of the mythopoeic movement of the unconscious and have come to appreciate it as a subcreative spiritual gift which brings recovery, escape, and consolation (Tolkien [1947] 1973). Yet the attitude I encountered in my sister prevails in many theological circles. One sees it, for example, in Karl Barth's veneration of Mozart's (supposed) objectivity, which denigrates the Romantic composers for their subjectivity or "personal confession" (1986, 37) as if this were somehow less Christian, and in Francis Schaeffer's (1976) *How Should We Then Live?*, which links self-expression to anarchy and equates fantasy with illusion, regarding all these as enemies of the church. These writers fail to satisfy my longings for an adequate theology because I cannot find meaning in the realm of the rational and material, and must seek it in intuition and imagination.

Pruyser (1968, 1974) highlights the significant relation between affect and meaning. He states that "to be orthodox is to be loved by our important orthodox love objects, to be considered lovable by them, and thus to have self-respect" (1968, 272). He regards "status dread," the concern with what others will think or say, as similarly motivated by the need for approval from those in authority. And he understands conformity and the resistance to change as rooted not only in the human preference for the familiar but also in the "emotional commitments which people have to a certain way of life as a whole pattern of interrelated values, even when some of these values are, strictly speaking, incompatible" (272). The price of letting go of such value systems is the sense of alienation, of being cut off from one's family, the loss of belongingness.

I have been fortunate in having a family more prone to expressing disapproval (although such expressing is often in a triangulated form) than to expelling. As the children in my family of origin have become adults, a variety of religious differences have been introduced, and my siblings are more tolerant than my parents would have been: we have survived divorce, cohabitation, conversion to Catholicism, the rejection of religion, a (temporary) shift to Unitarianism, and moves to other Protestant denominations. We judge, rather than debate, because of the strong tradition of looking to authorities to define what is right and wrong and because our Christian world view was not one that encouraged discrimination between shades of gray. Yet this same tradition taught us loyalty, and we remain rooted in a common heritage and language system, a legacy we can transform but not disown.

Implications for Family Therapy

Family therapists are evidencing an increasing concern with religious issues in family theory and therapy, a concern reflecting the larger culture's renewed interest in religion and a corresponding "return to respectability" for religious studies in academic circles (Winkler 1988). As millions of Americans become followers of "new religions," millions of others remain loyal to the traditional religions. A conservative estimate, based on various national polls, aligns at least 50% of the American population with the Judeo-Christian religions (see Jacquet 1984; Princeton Religion Research Center 1982; Quinn et al. 1982). This fact was taken into account by the most recent White House Conference on Families (1980), whose recommendations evidenced great sensitivity to religion, recognizing religious groups as significant support networks, including religion (along with culture, language, ethnicity, and economic concerns) as a significant source of differences between families, and supporting "the right of society through its community and public institutions to recognize the existence of a supreme being as long as specific faiths or denominations are not restricted or promoted" (98). As family-focused professionals increase their awareness of religion, churches struggle to develop a theology of the family that is informed by recent developments from family sociology and the family therapy fields (see Guernsey 1984; Rogers 1979). The goal is to develop a theology sensitive to the special problems of the 20th-century family and a family theory that takes seriously the Judeo-Christian world view (Salinger 1979).

It is definitely a boost to the Christian family, and to the Christian therapist, that the professional literature includes the receptiveness to the Christian world view evident in several recent writers. J. L. Griffith demonstrates insight into the assertion made by many Christians that "Christianity is not a religion, it is a *relationship*" (1986). Christians are involved in an interpersonal relationship with the divine, who becomes an additional person in the family's relational network, whose role is defined by both the family's dynamics and the religious tra-

dition. Christian life involves relationships vulnerable to isolation (from God and neighbor), healed by reunion (the processes
of confession and forgiveness), and fulfilled by communion
(Fitchett 1979); when therapy evokes these transcendent
moments, it may itself become a religious experience.

The family therapist's assessment model should include
inquiries about religious influences on every dimension, no matter which particular family theory is assumed. Illustrations of
this process can be found in the work of G. H. Zuk (1978), J. A.
Larsen (1978), and E. M. Pattison (1982), and in the analysis
presented in this chapter. An additional perspective on the complexity of such assessment comes from the model developed by
C. Glock (1962), who noted that religious research must take
into account at least five dimensions: the ideological (belief),
experiential (feeling), intellectual (knowledge), ritualistic (practice), and consequential (effects, both immediate and long-term).
One dimension is by no means entirely predictable from
another. For example, the "flower people" of the 1960s who
eventually became the "Jesus people" of the early 1970s adopted
the traditional ideology of their parents, but added entirely new
forms of worship and liturgy (Vande Kemp 1973). In the highly
religious culture of the 1980s and 1990s, there are many deeply
committed "new Christians" who are actively involved in worship (ritual) and experience (healing, charismatic renewal) and
are devout in their belief, but lacking in knowledge of both the
Bible and the confessions and history of the church. One can
seldom make assumptions in the ethical dimension (consequences), as issues such as abortion, euthanasia, divorce, sexual ethics, and homosexuality generate nearly as much discussion within the church as without it. Only the family therapist
attuned to the complex interweaving of all these dimensions—
religious and systemic—will gain an adequate appreciation of
the role of religion in the family and its potential for both patho-
genesis and healing.

References

Barker, F. G. 1988. Program notes to Gabriel Fauré, *Requiem*, op. 48.
Musical Heritage Society MHC 312135T.

Barth, K. 1986. *Wolfgang Amadeus Mozart*. Trans. C. K. Pott. Grand
Rapids: Eerdmans. Original German work published 1956.

Berger, M. M., ed. 1978. *Beyond the double bind: Communication and family systems, theories, and techniques with schizophrenia*. New York: Brunner/Mazel.

Carnival. 1941. In *The Catholic encyclopedic dictionary*, 171. New York: Gilmary Society.

Carnival. 1951. In *A Catholic dictionary*, ed. W. E. Addis and T. Arnold, rev. T. B. Scannell and P. E. Hallett, 118. 15th ed. London: Routledge and Kegan Paul.

Carter, B., and M. McGoldrick. 1988. 2d ed. *The changing family life cycle: A framework for family therapy*. New York: Gardner Press.

The comparative study Bible: A parallel Bible. 1984. Grand Rapids: Zondervan.

DeVries, A. 1961. *The children's Bible: The Holy Scripture as retold for children*. Trans. B. Fray and D. Rudston. St. Louis: Concordia. Published in 1978 as *Story Bible for young children* (Grand Rapids: Baker; St. Catherines, Ont.: Paideia Press).

Dykstra, D. I. 1983. *Who am I? and other sermons from Dimnent Memorial Chapel*. Holland, Mich.: Hope College.

Ecumenical creeds and Reformed confessions. 1987. Grand Rapids: CRC Publications.

Falicov, C. J., ed. 1988. *Family transitions: Continuity and change over the life cycle*. New York: Guilford Press.

Fitchett, G. A. 1979. Family therapy and communion. *Pastoral Psychology* 27:202–10.

Glock, C. 1962. On the study of religious commitment. *Religious Education* 42: S98–S110.

Goodwin, N. 1987. Program notes to Giuseppe Verdi, *Messa da requiem*. EMI Records CDS 549390.

Griffith, J. L. 1986. Employing the God-family relationship. *Family Process* 25:609–18.

Guernsey, D., ed. 1984. *Consultation on a theology of the family*. Pasadena, Calif.: Fuller Theological Seminary.

Hafner, R. J. 1986. *Marriage and mental illness: A sex roles perspective*. New York: Guilford Press.

Hiltner, S. 1972. *Theological dynamics*. Nashville: Abingdon.

Ho, M. K. 1987. Family therapy with ethnic minorities. Beverly Hills, Calif.: Sage.

Howard, T. [1976] 1979. *Splendour in the ordinary*. Reprinted as *Hallowed be this house*. Wheaton: Shaw Publications.

Jacquet, C. H., Jr. 1984. *Yearbook of American and Canadian churches 1984.* Nashville: Abingdon.

Kantor, D., and W. Lehr. [1975] 1976. *Inside the family: Toward a theory of family process.* [San Francisco: Jossey-Bass.] Reprint. New York: Harper.

Kross, S. n.d. Program notes to Johannes Brahms, *German requiem,* op. 45. Deutsche Grammophon Gesellschaft recording 2832 006.

Larsen, J. A. 1978. Dysfunction in the evangelical family. *Family Coordinator* 27:261–67.

L'Engle, M. 1962. *A wrinkle in time.* New York: Farrar, Straus and Giroux.

———. 1973. *A wind in the door.* New York: Farrar, Straus and Giroux.

———. 1978. *A swiftly tilting planet.* New York: Farrar, Straus and Giroux.

Lewis, C. S. [1947] 1973. On stories. In *Essays presented to Charles Williams,* ed. C. S. Lewis, 90–105. [Oxford: Oxford University Press.] Grand Rapids: Eerdmans.

McGoldrick, M., J. K. Pearce, and J. Giordano, eds. 1982. *Ethnicity and family therapy.* New York: Guilford Press.

Office of the General Assembly. 1983. *The constitution of the Presbyterian Church (U.S.A.). Part 1, Book of confessions.* New York.

———. 1986–87. *The constitution of the Presbyterian Church (U.S.A.). Part 2, Book of order.* New York.

Pattison, E. M. 1982. Management of religious issues in family therapy. *International Journal of Family Therapy* 4:140–63.

Pittman, Frank S. 1987. *Turning points: Treating families in transition and crisis.* New York: Norton.

Princeton Religion Research Center. 1982. *Religion in America.* Princeton. N. J.

Pruyser, P. W. 1968. *A dynamic psychology of religion.* New York: Harper and Row.

———. 1974. *Between belief and unbelief.* New York: Harper and Row.

Quinn, B., H. Anderson, M. Bradley, P. Goetting, and P. Shriver, eds. 1982. *Churches and church membership in the United States 1980: An enumeration by region, state, and county on data reported by 111 church bodies.* Atlanta: Glenmary Research Center (for the National Council of Churches of Christ in the U.S.A.).

Rogers, J. 1985. *The Presbyterian creeds: A guide to the "Book of Confessions."* Philadelphia: Westminster.

Rogers, M. L. 1979. Some Bible families examined from a systems perspective. *Journal of Psychology and Theology* 7:251–58.

Salinger, R. J. 1979. Toward a biblical framework for family therapy. *Journal of Psychology and Theology* 7:241–50.

Schaeffer, F. A. 1976. *How should we then live? The rise and decline of Western thought and culture.* Old Tappan, N. J.: Revell.

Schiappa, B. D. 1982. *Mixing Catholic-Protestant marriages in the 1980s: A guidebook for couples and families.* Ramsey, N. J.: Paulist Press.

Tolkien, J. R. R. [1947] 1973. On fairy-stories. In *Essays presented to Charles Williams*, ed. C. S. Lewis, 106–27. [Oxford: Oxford University Press.] Grand Rapids: Eerdmans.

Vandehulst, W. G. 1963. *The big read-to-me story book.* Grand Rapids: Zondervan. Published in 1978 as *My favorite story book*, trans. M. Schoolland. St. Catherines, Ont.: Paideia Press.

Vande Kemp, H. 1973. Dimensions of religious growth and development in the college years. Master's thesis, University of Massachusetts, Amherst.

———. 1987. Relational ethics in the novels of Charles Williams. *Family Process* 26:283–94.

Vande Kemp, H., and G. P. Schreck. 1981. The church's ministry to singles: A family model. *Journal of Religion and Health* 20:141–55.

White House Conference on Families. 1980. *Listening to America's families. Action for the '80s. The report to the president, Congress, and families of the nation.* Washington, D.C.

Winawer-Steiner, H., and N. A. Wetzel. 1982. German families. In *Ethnicity and family therapy*, ed. M. McGoldrick, J. K. Pearce, and J. Giordano, 247–68. New York: Guilford Press.

Winkler, K. J. 1988. After years in academic limbo, the study of religion undergoes a revival of interest among scholars. *Chronicle of Higher Education* 34 (21, 3 February): A4–A7.

Zuk, G. H. 1978. A therapist's perspective on Jewish family values. *Journal of Marriage and Family Counseling* 4:103–10.

3

Personhood and Relational Life Tasks

A Model for Integrating Psychology and Theology

G. Peter Schreck

The Relational Life Tasks (RLT) model, a paradigm for understanding persons and personal behavior, is one that integrates my thought and work as a student and teacher of family systems theory, as a member of a seminary faculty, and as a clinician with nearly a decade of practice devoted to marriage and family therapy. I find it difficult to remember the precise sequence in which I synthesized this diverse yet intertwined background, but clearly my thoughts began to crystalize as I attempted to categorize the diverse concerns that prompted my clients to seek therapy. Whether I listened to individuals, couples, or families, the multiplicity of their specific issues clustered around four questions: (*a*) Who am I? (*b*) To whom am I close? (or, who is close to me?) (*c*) What am I to do with my life? and (*d*) How will I be whole (or saved)? In turn, I equated these four questions with the concerns of *identity, intimacy, industry,* and *integrity,* respectively. Of

77

course clients seldom used these terms, for they were my formulations. They did seem, however, to correspond, without being arbitrary or artificially superimposed, to the clients' wrestlings and explorations.

Having the categories, or questions, in mind began to help me identify more quickly—and at times more accurately—the issues with which my clients were concerned. Thus, the four recurring questions provided the basis for a differential diagnosis. More than once, a case that was presented initially in terms that suggested difficulty in one category was actually understood, and processed, better when seen as relating to one of the other categories. For example, a presenting complaint of not feeling close to one's spouse turned out to be an expression of dissatisfaction with a job that did not adequately fill the need for doing something meaningful with one's life. Working actively with the four categories has enabled me to listen in a more sensitive and perceptive manner as my clients have attempted to formulate their areas of pain and growth.

But not only as a therapist have the categories been useful to me. As a seminary professor teaching in the area of pastoral care, I have found the four categories, or questions, to embrace what it means to think about personal and relational dynamics from a theological perspective. I can hardly think of more basic spiritual concerns than those inherent in the four formulated questions. Hence, in my seminary teaching and in my ongoing attempt to relate constructively my Christian faith to my work as a marriage and family therapist, the four basic themes have emerged as a promising locus of integrating my own theological and psychological commitments.

Relational Life Tasks Model:
Overview and Definitions

It requires work to be and become a person. Much of the work is our own; part of it belongs to others who are related to us in some way. And the work continues throughout our lives. Because this is so, it makes sense to speak of *relational life tasks*. Let me elaborate upon each of the three words, beginning with the last.

The notion of *tasks* that pertains here is captured in the observation, made by the German theologian Helmut Thielicke, that to be a person is both *Gabe* (gift) and *Aufgabe* (assigned task). To be born, as indicated in the phrase "to be given" life, captures the gift dimension of being (though even here someone else needed to work, or "labor"). And ample hereditary endowment is referred to as "being gifted." Once these gifts have been taken into account, however, there is little doubt that to be and to grow up requires considerable effort. The truth is that, in the realm of personhood, there simply isn't much "instant" anything. Complex organisms never begin life mature—neither physically nor psychically. Instead, they always begin immature, or incomplete, and reach maturity only through mastering certain steps. In other words, it takes work! Thus, no matter what we have been given (*Gabe*), mature personhood can only be achieved through the accomplishing of particular, existentially assigned tasks (*Aufgaben*). More specifically, the essential tasks required of us relate to the four questions previously cited. Each question corresponds to a significant human concern: (*a*) "Who am I?" corresponds to *gaining self*; (*b*) "To whom am I close?" raises the issue of *sharing self*; (*c*) "What am I to do with my life?" relates to *investing self*; and (*d*) "How will I be whole?" is associated with *saving self*. Finding and fashioning personal answers to each question is at the core of one's being a person. Doing so is to be engaged in the tasks of being and becoming a self.

Though the efforts at being and becoming are tasks, it is more appropriate to think of them as *life tasks* because they continue to be a person's responsibility and challenge throughout the course of his or her life. In this regard the RLT model has a certain similarity to the developmental concepts of theorists such as Erik Erikson (1950), Daniel Levinson (1978), and Elizabeth Carter and Monica McGoldrick (1980). There is an important difference, however, between the way these theorists approach the matter of life tasks, or stages, and the way they are conceptualized here. Rather than see the tasks as sequential over the life span, I find it more helpful to think about the tasks as essentially cybernetic, that is, as mutually interacting with and influencing each other. Thus, while Erikson (1950) proposed the concept of "epigenetic stages" to indicate that an individual can move to a subsequent stage only upon successful completion of the essential task inherent in the previous one and while Carter and McGoldrick (1980) speak of developmental stages as "horizontal stressors" in family life, I prefer a less linear formulation to depict the dynamics that exist between these deeply personal tasks. For example, in real life what we do has an impact on who we think we are—and vice versa. A reciprocal relation exists between efforts at gaining self and at investing self. And precisely because such reciprocity exists between all of the tasks involved in being and becoming, and because it continues throughout life, it is appropriate to designate the tasks as life tasks.

When the adjective *relational* is affixed to the term *life tasks*, it affirms the notion that to be and to become a person is inherently a process that takes place through relationships. Essentially this means that none of the life tasks can be accomplished by a person individually. In spite of the formulation of each task in terms of "self," the focus is not on individual dynamics but on interpersonal ones. In this regard, the RLT model reflects a systems orientation, and the relationship system of particular significance for these aspects of selfhood is the family.

To complete this overview, figure 3.1 provides a graphic representation of the RLT paradigm. Well-suited for depicting certain aspects of the model, the tetrahedron offers four distinct points that, nevertheless, form a whole. The relationship among the points is not purely linear, that is, they cannot be connected by a single line; rather, the relationship is compatible with a dynamic for growth in one or more of the parts as well as in the whole. Moreover, the shape of a tetrahedron roughly corresponds to that of a helix (i.e., its volume can be filled by the helix). This correspondence is particularly intriguing in light of the Wynnes' (1986) suggestion that a helix more accurately reflects the developmental nature of personal growth than does a linear model. Furthermore, no necessary priority is given to any of the vertices in a tetrahedron, which is consistent with the cybernetic dynamic among the various tasks. In other words, the paradigm itself does not indicate that one of the tasks has priority over the others.

Components of the Model: Four Tasks

Identity

The relational life task inherent in the notion of identity is the work of gaining "self." Admittedly, each person exists as a

Figure 3.1 **Relational Life Tasks Model**

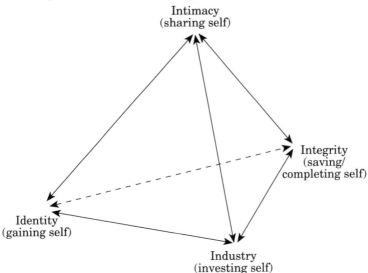

self from the moment of birth, or sooner, but probably has no awareness of this reality until quite some time later. (At any rate, I have no recollection of these early days.) Although the fascinating work of object relations theorists (St. Clair 1986) has suggested that infants are decidedly more active psychologically than had previously been thought, this only underscores the contention that to become conscious of being a self—to gain a sense of selfhood—is a task that awaits the newborn. It simply is not something bequeathed at birth.

The specific aspects involved in the task comprise many of the fundamental notions of personal psychology. Gaining self, among other things, means discovering personal boundaries. It means learning that our bodies are not coterminous with the world, that the body's perimeter is established by the skin. And gaining a sense of self necessitates becoming familiar with, and owning, what is contained inside that skin. Identity, at the very least, means coming to terms with the fact that one is a body (putting it this way reflects a more biblical perspective than saying that "one has a body"). Identity involves what Ernest Becker (1973) terms "body seating," which implies becoming comfortable with the assets and liabilities of the physical self.

The degree to which we manage this has significant implications for our self-esteem—a notion which, while not synonymous with identity, has significant bearing upon it. How we embrace our bodies' characteristics and potentials (looks, sexual functioning, finitude), reflects on our sense of self.

Equally important as discovering physical boundaries and owning bodily characteristics are the corresponding tasks related to the psychological self. This involves learning that our cognitions, feelings, desires, and preferences are in some sense always uniquely ours. While others may share some of these with us, their thoughts and feelings are not ours. It is in recognizing our mental, emotional, and volitional realities that we learn something of who we are. And in the claiming of these realities as our own, we begin to gain self. Murray Bowen's concept of differentiation of self, which is characterized by an increase of "basic self" over "pseudo self," addresses this issue: "The basic self is a definite quality illustrated by such 'I position' stances as: 'These are my beliefs and convictions. This is what I am, and who I am, and what I will do, or not do.' The basic self may be changed from *within* self on the basis of new knowledge and experience" (1978, 473). But such a sense of the self, according to Bowen, is achieved through deliberate and demanding psychological work. Differentiation of self, or gaining basic self, is the task of identity. It is fashioning a statement of who we are.

Before considering the relational life task of sharing self, or intimacy, and as a transition to it, I want to address identity in terms of one of the earliest responses we learn as an answer to the question, "Who are you?" That response is our names. It is interesting how much significance is given to a name and to its use. When we as young children made a connection between ourselves and our names, this represented an emerging self-awareness on our part—the same self-awareness that is measured when we, as adults, are asked to give our names in a basic mental-status exam. Others assume we know who we are, at some level at least, when we can name ourselves. But is such an assumption valid? Surely our ability to parrot the two or three proper nouns we hear others use in referring to us does not guarantee that we have any real sense of our identities. Yet behind the purely reflexive use of our names in response to the question "Who are you?" stands a profound truth about who we are, for the universal convention of naming serves as a code for the two essential components of personal identity: namely, a sense of belonging and a sense of separateness. Salvador Minuchin (1974) maintains that these two indispensable aspects of the human experience are provided above all by the family, which he terms "the matrix of identity" precisely because in the family is where the experiences of separateness and belonging take place first and foremost. And it is to that reality of both belonging and being separate that our names point. Our last names (or family names) indicate to which family we *belong,* while our first names (or given names) affirm that we are *separate*, or unique, in the relational context.

The precise balance between belonging and separateness that we experienced in our families necessarily contributes to the sense of self that we have today. In other words, the matter of identity, while very personal, is not individualistic but relational. Ultimately, gaining self is not something we do by ourselves alone, but it occurs primarily within the context of our relationships. That is what makes identity a relational life task—and makes identity impossible without intimacy.

Intimacy

If identity is gaining self, then intimacy amounts to sharing self. It requires both sharing aspects of our selves with another, and having the other feel free to do the same with us. Moreover, the distinction made by Mark Schaefer and David Olson between intimacy as *experience* and intimacy as *relationship* adds significantly to the definition, for the latter assumes that the sharing will be both extensive and recurring: "While intimate experiences are elusive and unpredictable phenomena that may occur spontaneously, an intimate relationship may take time, work and effort to maintain" (1981, 50). Hence, intimacy, as defined here, involves the mutual giving and receiving of selves within an established relational context.

As the self-giver, being intimate with another means that we make our personal boundaries more permeable so that the other can come closer to knowing and encountering our selves. Our thoughts, feelings, hopes—those inner aspects of who we are that another cannot know unless we reveal them—those we choose to share with the other. Similarly, intimacy may involve giving to the other access to our physical selves via proximity, touch, or sexual relating. And the sharing of our emotional selves happens as we give the other a place of existential significance in our lives, as evidenced by our attitudes of vulnerability, commitment, and respect. In the role of receiver, we let the other give his or her self to us in the same way. Genuine intimacy requires that the giving and receiving be mutual, comparable, and recurring. The specifics, or the content, of what is shared need not be identical, but the process of sharing must be mutually embraced.

From this understanding of intimacy as the mutual giving and receiving of selves, it follows that identity is necessary for intimacy. If we do not know who we are—if we have gained no self—we will have no self to share. As Erikson observed, "It is only after a reasonable sense of identity has been established that real intimacy with the other sex (or, for that matter, with any other person or even with oneself) is possible" (1980, 101). (And just letting someone else share his or her self with us [i.e., being good listeners or quiet supporters who let the other carry the conversation] will never yield intimacy, precisely because intimacy requires the mutual sharing of selves.) But lest it seem that identity has priority among the relational life tasks, remember that identity is impossible without intimacy. More than simply being an objective exchange of information, genuine sharing of self (intimacy) results in gaining self (identity). Put another way, we never really know who we are without the opportunity of seeing our selves reflected in the other with whom we are intimate.

Industry

Identity and intimacy are psychological staples; industry, the third relational life task, has not received the same attention from psychologists. This inattention is all the more surprising since early on Freud observed that people need to love *and work*. Yet, somehow, psychology has spent much more effort examining what it means for a person to love than for a person to work—even though most people probably see themselves spending more time working than loving. However that may be, in the RLT model the issue of work comes under the rubric of industry. Industry raises the question of what we are to do with our lives. It deals with the task of investing self. The need to work, to accomplish something, appears to be deeply rooted in personhood. Indeed, in *Modern Work and Human Meaning*, John Raines and Donna Day-Lower define work as "human living—human being and human becoming" (1986, 15). Far beyond economic necessity, the urge to be productive, to get a job, or to pursue a career reflects a basic personal need that we must attempt to meet. Finding a satisfactory way to express that urge and meet that need constitutes another life task. And, just as identity and intimacy, industry does prove to be a task. Often that "satisfactory way" is not initially obvious: it remains to be discovered, needs to be prepared for, has to be practiced. Sometimes the way to express the urge needs to be revised, either by choice or by necessity. But clearly, learning how and where to invest one's self—and doing so—is a lifelong task.

The relational nature of the task of investing self is reflected in the character and goal of work. Raines and Day-Lower elaborate upon this as follows:

> Work remains . . . a unique human dignity and the expression of a unique human connectedness—a gift each human gives to every other human and each generation gives to the next. Precisely by our working we should be drawn out of our narrow self-preoccupation and excessive self-regard into that clarity of self-perception which sees our common human journey, nourished by the creativity and sacrifice of those who labored here before us. We should be reminded that we too are part of this journey—that our time is a part of all time, and that as inheritors we are also responsible to preserve and add to this legacy, which is built up and made fruitful in human labor. (1986, 17)

The self-investment of industry, when viewed from this perspective, is not something we do for ourselves alone, but something that has meaning as a consequence of the relational reality of our lives. Our work, originating in our sense of self, is thus an expression of intimacy. We share our selves (especially our abilities and creative resources) with others. Lester De Koster captured the intimacy inherent in work when he observed, "Work is essentially a gift, the gift of the self to the service of others" (1982, 82).

Industry, as the investing of self, need not be limited to the domain of the marketplace. There are other areas in which we can invest our selves with the goal of contributing part of our legacy to others. Especially when the "others" are the next generation living under our roofs, a critical way to invest our selves in them is through the work of parenting. What better captures the essence of human connectedness, of being drawn out of narrow self-preoccupation and excessive self-regard and of being fellow travelers on the common human journey, than the rigors of laboring as an effective parent? To be sure, the experience of parenting does not belong to the domain of industry alone, for it offers opportunities for profound intimacy and self-discovery. However, parenting certainly cannot be understood as anything less than significant investing of self. As any parent will attest—parenting is work.

Integrity

Erikson (1950) used the term *integrity* to designate the final stage of the life cycle, in which the focus is upon life review and the recognition of meaning in the life the individual has lived. His designation is narrower than, but not inconsistent with, the use of the term in the RLT model. In essence, the task of integrity involves becoming whole through the discovery, acceptance, and nurturance of our selves as spiritual beings. Integrity, therefore, has to do with spirituality.

What, at the end of the 20th century, is spirituality? It can mean everything from new-age faith in the therapeutic power of crystals, to a holistic (though basically humanistic) appreciation of the ecological system of planet earth, to a radical belief in a transcendent and personal God whose existence is of consequence to humankind. While there is much in the history of psychology to suggest that the discipline is not particularly compatible with the last, and more traditional, understanding of spirituality, precisely there is where we must find the answer not only to the question of the meaning of our lives (à la Erikson) but also to the question of what constitutes wholeness, or salvation. This is a larger question, for it has immediate, as well as teleological, significance for us as people.

Admittedly, in the RLT model integrity has a theological nuance. But that is only as it should be when we believe that we, as humans, stand in relationship to a transcendent and personal God. When we confess this God as Creator, as Redeemer, and as Lord, we make profound statements not only about God but also about our selves. We affirm our identity as created and existentially dependent beings; we acknowledge the potential we have for intimacy with God; and we recognize our industry to be the investing of personal resources and abilities in the created order that God decreed. Spirituality thus conceived is indeed theological, but on that basis it need not be psychologically suspect.

As do the quests for identity, intimacy, and industry, the pursuit of integrity occurs only, and always, in the interpersonal context of my self and a personal God, that is, a God who is a person. It is a task, for it does not happen automatically. Accepting that we are spiritual beings and acting on that—letting that be part of our sense of self—also comes about only through sustained effort and discipline. Richard Foster (1978) offers one of the most compelling statements to that effect in *Celebration of Discipline*. Similarly, integrity must also be understood as relational. It occurs only, and always, in interpersonal contexts (God is understood as personal). True spirituality is not autonomous. And saving self is a life task, meaning that it invites participation throughout all of life. To be sure, the task of saving self contributes to an end-stage life review and search for meaning; it may even be seen as life's ultimate goal and gain. But pursuit of wholeness and salvation does not need to be deferred until the end of life.

While integrity has certain characteristics in common with identity, intimacy, and industry, it is also qualitatively different from them. Let me explain. Identity, intimacy, and industry can be conceptualized as three corners of a triangle, as in Stephen Marks's (1986) *Three Corners*. In fact, when I first began to think about the relational life tasks, I used a schema that represented wholeness or salvation as resulting from a balanced interplay between these three components of life (see figure 3.2). But the two-dimensional model was inadequate, for integrity, or spirituality, cannot rightly be reduced to the sum of good human interactions. By introducing integrity as a discrete fourth task, I not only avoid this reductionism but also more accurately reflect the reality of human existence; namely, that spirituality is yet another dimension of life and one that has a qualitative impact upon all other aspects of living. The current paradigm, in which the two-dimensional triangle has been replaced by the three-dimensional tetrahedron,[1] more

---

1. I am indebted to the Reverend John Zellner for the specific notion of the tetrahedron. It was in his reaction to an earlier form of my Relational Life Tasks model that he pointed me toward this helpful construct.

Figure 3.2 **Two-dimensional Representation of the Relational Life Tasks Model**

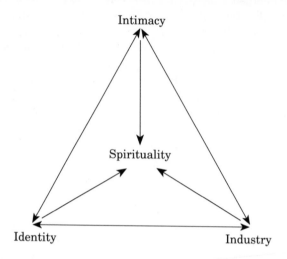

adequately depicts the relational life tasks and—especially—the dynamics inherent *within* and *among* them.

The Dynamics of the Model

Two basic dynamics energize the RLT model. One is developmental, and the other is systemic, or cybernetic. The former pertains more to what happens within the tasks themselves, while the latter focuses primarily on the interaction between and among them. And while the two dynamics are distinct, in real life they converge. Only in an artificial context, such as an essay, can they actually be treated separately.

Developmental Process

We do not begin life with a completed or mature version of any aspect of our selves. More likely, we have no notion at all of such things as self, others, work, or God. But we do have the potential—perhaps even an inner necessity—to discover and relate to each of these realities. The process by which this potential is realized is the phenomenon of growth via change. The latent becomes actual; the rudimentary evolves into the mature; the child becomes the adult. This dynamic, to the extent that it is operational in each of the four relational life tasks, contributes to the development of personhood.

To be and become a self requires development within each of the four tasks of identity, intimacy, industry, and integrity. Perhaps this fact is rather self-evident and does not raise many issues, but does such a developmental schema best explain the relationship that exists between the respective tasks? For some it does. The concept of development into adulthood through life stages has been touted by poet, philosopher, and scientist alike. Within the social science ranks, Erikson (1950) and Levinson (1978) are particularly prominent exponents of this perspective. Yet when it comes to the interaction between the tasks, such a developmental dynamic, because of its inherently sequential or linear nature, is inadequate. Debating the merits of a theory of epigenetic stages is beyond the scope of this chapter. Let me simply reiterate that although developmental dynamics are operative *within* each task, they do not adequately account for the relationship *among* the relational life tasks.

Essential here is the distinction between relational life tasks and developmental stages. In spite of similarities in nomenclature, the relational life tasks presented here are not to be equated with the epigenetic stages of a developmentalist like Erikson. Two important considerations support the distinction. First, gaining self (identity) is a task, not a stage. It cannot be a stage because it is a lifelong task. (But because it does occur over the duration of one's life, growth—or development—within this task is both possible and necessary. The same holds true for intimacy, industry, and integrity.) Second, one task does not lead to a subsequent one, or, stated another way, completion of one task is not the prerequisite for beginning another. This constitutes a radical departure from the conventional developmentalist assumption. Central to this divergence is the rejection of the linear model in favor of a cybernetic, or systemic, one.

Cybernetics

To speak of cybernetics is to speak of reciprocity. More than development within a task over time (maturation), and rather than one task's completion leading to the initiation of a subsequent one (linear causality), the essential dynamic of the RLT

Figure 3.3 Reciprocal Interactions among the Relational Life Tasks

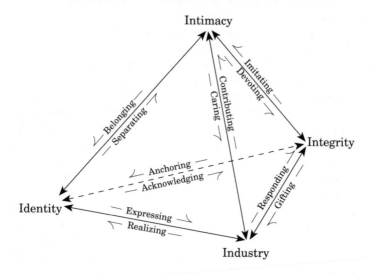

model is found in the reciprocal relationships posited between the tasks. It is not just that identity and intimacy, for example, mutually affect each other. Instead, each one of the four tasks has a reciprocal relation with the other three. Figure 3.3 schematizes the function of these multiple and reciprocal interactions with six sets of double arrows (pointing in opposite directions) that connect each of the vertices of the tetrahedron with each other. A brief description of these six sets of cybernetic connections follows. (There is no necessary starting point; the choice is arbitrary.)

Belonging—separating. The interaction between identity and intimacy consists of experiences of belonging and separating. Object relations theorists (St. Clair 1986) have elaborated upon the alternating successions of connections and separations that characterize human life and make the point that precisely this dialectic stands at the center of the process of being and becoming a self. Conception and birth reflect this dynamic, but so do all subsequent efforts at self-definition, self-knowledge, and self-realization. We gain our selves only as we are with, and separate from, others—especially significant others. Through repeated interactions with familial subsystems in which we either find ourselves included or excluded, we begin to fashion our identities. We learn how we are like, and how we are different from, parents, siblings, males, females, athletes, musicians, extroverts, and others. We find we have feelings and thoughts that others also have, and some that seem to be uniquely ours. And through this process of comparing and contrasting, a sense of self emerges.

The same dynamic of belonging and separating also fashions our experience of intimacy. If intimacy is the task of sharing self, then it requires that we have an awareness of our separateness, for it is primarily out of that awareness that we know we have anything to share. But even while we have a need to share out of our sense of separateness, we are sensitive to the degree of belonging—whether actual or potential—that exists between ourselves and others. Belonging also determines our willingness and ability to share self. Too little, as well as too much, belongingness impedes the process of establishing intimacy. Both possibilities are problematic. An absence of a sense of belonging militates against sharing self; an overabundance of togetherness has the same result. These are the polarities that Minuchin (1974) calls disengagement and enmeshment and that Bowen (1978) identifies as emotional cut-off and fusion. Ivan Boszormenyi-Nagy and Geraldine Spark (1973) point to the same realities with their notion of relational entitlements and obligations, both of which can be either absent or too powerful.

In the extreme, disengagement, cut-off, and lack of entitlement characterize an emotional environment in which the sharing of self is perceived as too risky for the self's survival. Without the security of a reciprocal belonging, separating is death (for ultimately death is separation). On the other hand, enmeshment, fusion, and extreme loyalty obligations make the sharing of self impossible because under these conditions the self as a distinct being does not exist. The self has been swallowed up by the other, to whom it belongs totally, or as Virginia Satir (1972) describes it, the self has been "crossed out" in favor of the other.

In contrast to the extreme forms of separating and belonging stands a cybernetic interplay between these two realities, which sets up a dynamic that permits both the gaining of self and the sharing of self. Through related interactions with those whose dependable availability communicates that we belong to them, we become cognizant of who we are. The significant others function as a mirror that lets us see our selves. In light of what we see, and in light of their trustworthiness (i.e., they have not wanted to either possess us or destroy us), it becomes possible for us to affirm as well as to change what we see. And the more we choose to expose our selves to that mirror, the more we can come to know our selves. In this way, sharing self (willingness to stand in front of others openly) contributes to gaining self. But it also works the other way around. Having a clearer sense of who we are permits us to share more of our selves, for we can only share what we have. Moreover, our ability to let another share his or her self with us (the other dimension of intimacy) also requires that our selves be sufficiently defined to avoid the possible pitfalls of either engulfing or being engulfed by the other. In other words, identity is a sine qua non for intimacy, and only to the degree to which we have gained self will we be able to have experiences of genuine and growing intimacy.

Realizing—expressing. Identity and industry are linked in the reciprocal dynamic of realizing self and expressing self. Conceptualizing the link in this way challenges an all-too-common misconception, namely, that who I am is what I do or what I do determines who I am. Who I am and what I do are intimately connected, but not in the way that many people assume when they answer the question "Who are you?" by first giving their name and then indicating the type of work they do. No, the relationship between identity and industry cannot be reduced to an equation. Instead, the RLT model posits that identity finds expression in industry. Work is the way we invest our abilities and gifts in the performance of some task. At its best, work provides a means by which we demonstrate our creative and productive qualities. It is a way through which we make our selves known—express our selves.

The ultimately human dimension gives work its essential worth and dignity and makes the investing of self such a significant personal process. Yet the significance inheres not only in the fact that through investing self we express our selves, but also that through industry we discover our selves in unique ways. It is a distortion of this important connection that lies behind mistakenly equating industry with identity. We are not what we do; to assert otherwise is an overstatement. But what we do does contribute to our sense of self, both by letting us see some external expression of our selves (recognition) and also by enabling us to realize our selves (actualization). Realizing self, therefore, necessitates incorporating into our self-concept as actual that which before was only potential. Thus, industry has the ability to expand our sense of self, as well as stifle it. Job success or job satisfaction can contribute to our self-esteem, while underemployment or unemployment can represent serious threats to our sense of self (Raines and Day-Lower 1986). Through the reciprocal dynamics of expressing and realizing self, identity and industry quite clearly influence each other.

Contributing—caring. The manner in which intimacy and industry impinge upon each other may seem less obvious than the interconnectedness that exists between either identity and intimacy or identity and industry. Nevertheless, what connects intimacy and industry is an important reciprocal dynamic, to which Freud alluded when he insisted that every person has the need to love and to work. Though it is possible to see these as two totally unrelated needs, it may be more accurate to view love and work as opposite sides of the same coin.

True work—work actually fulfilling the deep human need to be a worker—is effort we expend that contributes in some fashion to another's life experience. Our need to work, therefore, cannot be met by simply being occupied; work has to have a goal or purpose. Nor is it enough for our labor to serve essentially self-directed goals. To be sure, industry does meet the personal need of realizing/expressing self. But such an individualistic objective does not adequately explain the phenomenon of human labor. Rather the need to contribute, to build upon what others have already contributed to the human enterprise of constructing a civilization, lies behind our need to invest our selves through the use of time, talents, and energy. In this sense, industry is radically a *relational* life task. In the final analysis, work is that which we know we have done for our fellows, the truth of which seems to be reflected—even if often in grossly distorted fashion—in the notion that work deserves pay. Payment (in whatever currency) bears testimony that not only we, but others also, recognize our labor as having been done for others and, therefore, having worth.

The notion of contributing, or sharing, with others via work is only part of the connection between industry and intimacy. It highlights how industry qualitatively defines intimacy, but the dynamic is reciprocal. Intimacy, in turn, infuses work with a quality best described as *caring*. When work is conceived as a means of being close to others—as a way of sharing our selves with them— then the manner in which we do our work is affected. Moreover, the very nature of our work stands to be affected by this connection. Thus, undertakings that belie intimacy may well become unacceptable work options for us. Positions that exploit, products intended to destroy, procedures that dehumanize, and objectives that discount the other are rejected as valid expressions of industry because they are basically incompatible with intimacy. They do not promote the sharing of selves; instead, the pursuit of such work results in alienation and conflict. Conversely, when labor conforms to the goal of expressing care for others, when both how the work is done and what is done contribute to the realization of that basic human need to share one's self with another, then work is a way of loving—of making society intimate.

Anchoring—acknowledging. The reciprocal dynamic between integrity and identity deals with anchoring and acknowledging. In the task of gaining self, spirituality functions to anchor the self in a reality that transcends the individual. Within a Christian framework, this means specifically that our sense of self is informed by the existence of a personal God on whom our existence depends. Thus, the work of gaining self can be undertaken not only with the possibility but also with the necessity that it will involve a relationship with God. In fact, any effort to discover our selves apart from such a relationship is ultimately seen as inadequate. Hence, a concept as basic as anchoring aptly describes the impact upon gaining self that comes with the recognition of the integrity component. Anchoring significantly informs such identity issues as our self-worth, reason for being, and place in the scheme of things. There can be no more radical grounding of our identity than in the sense of self gained through a relationship with God.

If integrity provides anchoring for the self in the ultimate reality of God via a personal relationship, then what reciprocal contribution does identity make? Despite the role of spirituality to anchor our sense of personhood in the transcendence of godhood, it lies within our power to acknowledge the realm of the spiritual and its role in our quest for salvation (integrity). This does not make acknowledging the same as creating. We do not create the spiritual; it is not the product of our imagination or our inner fears and needs. (The difference between acknowledging and creating is also that which distinguishes faith from fantasy and religious experience from blatant psychosis.) And yet, without the personal acknowledgment of God's significance for us, there is a sense in which God does not exist for us. Without acknowledging God, we can experience no anchoring of our selves in spiritual reality. On the other hand, through our acknowledgment of God ("belief in God" and "trust in God" are other ways of saying the same thing), there comes into existence a relationship with God, which contributes to our gaining self as we experience separateness and belongingness in the relationship.

Imitating—devoting. The manner in which concern for wholeness, or integrity, influences the task of sharing self with others is called *imitating*. To be open to finding wholeness through experiencing God in our lives is to be open to experiencing intimacy. Within a Christian framework, God lets us know who God is through self-disclosure, or revelation. The essence of revelation, of course, is precisely what intimacy is, namely, the sharing of self with another. This process of sharing self stands in sharp contrast to the concept of being discovered. We do not discover God any more than we create spirituality. Instead, in God's self-disclosure we encounter intimacy—the intimacy inherent in the process as well as in the content of revelation.

Our response to God's intimate initiative can be either withdrawal or the sharing of our selves in return. The latter response is imitation. Learning to share our selves with God creates in us the spiritual dimension essential to integrity, namely, intimate relatedness with God. Moreover, imitating is a relational response that we can also employ with others. In effect, integrity contributes to the relational life task of intimacy to the degree to which we imitate God by being willing to initiate disclosure of our selves to others—whether to God or human beings.

But intimacy also has a bearing on integrity. Sharing of self contributes to the task of seeking wholeness. It does so particularly through the process of esteeming God. What this entails is highlighted in a familiar phrase from the Shorter Catechism of the Westminster Confession, which asserts that "man's chief end . . . is to glorify God and to enjoy him forever." Here the achievement of our intended purpose as human beings (integrity) is clearly equated with expressing love and devotion toward God, that is, being intimate with God. This intimacy is often operationalized through God-directed behaviors of devotion such as worship and prayer. As we engage in these expressions of intimacy toward God, however, we acknowledge not only the reality of a spiritual realm "out there" but also the reality of a spiritual realm within our own selves. In effect, we realize (meaning "make real") aspects of our person precisely as we practice that of which we are capable. Thus, sharing self via religious behaviors that express our devotion to God contributes to the development of our selves as spiritual beings.

Gifting—responding. The final instance of a reciprocal interaction within the RLT model pertains to the integrity-industry dynamic. One tenet of Christian spirituality is that we are gifted by God's Spirit with particular graces (*charismata*) that enable us to perform particular tasks or functions with divine enablement. Hence, the relational life task of seeking wholeness must include personally coming to terms with the particular endowment received from God. One aspect of this coming to terms involves recognizing and accepting our spiritual dimension—and the relationship with God that the dimension implies. By virtue of being gifted by God, we cannot adequately understand our selves apart from either the gift or the giver. And to understand our selves as beings related to God in this manner has particular relevance for our industry. Indeed, to address the question of what we are to do with our lives—to seek to invest our selves—without acknowledging the spiritual reality of being gifted for a particular task would be to foreclose on our wholeness. To do so would mean to ignore a significant dimension of our person.

However, recognizing the gifting of God, and the enabling for work which it entails, is but one aspect of the integrity-industry dynamic. The other part of the reciprocal interaction involves how we actually invest our selves. When our work constitutes a response to God's gifting, then our work contributes to our wholeness, or salvation.[2] Of course, our industry does not do so in the sense of making us deserving of salvation, as if we had earned it; rather, our work accomplishes our wholeness. When we act in accordance with our giftedness, we act in a manner that is consistent with who, and how, God has made us to be. We are in a right relationship with God at a functional level. Indeed, such behavioral correspondence with our spiritual constitution is the essence of integrity.

Theological Amplification

The four basic questions that the RLT model addresses are inherently theological in nature. Indeed, these four basic issues concerning the self belong as much to the domain of theology as they do to the province of psychology. Admittedly, the language used by the two disciplines varies decidedly, but the substance of what is being discussed is really quite similar, and even the answers arrived at by good psychology and sound theology can be remarkably alike. The similarity is what I propose to establish here, by looking specifically at how the relational life tasks of gaining, sharing, investing, and completing self are deeply anchored in the theological concepts of creation, incarnation, redemption, and the kingdom of God.

Creation

Theology answers the question of who we are with the assertion that we are persons created in the image of God. The concept of *imago dei* has been variously developed by theologians, but the biblical text from which this construct emerges—and therefore, the crucial one for understanding it—is the familiar creation account of Genesis 1:26–31. With disarming direct-

2. When referring to a person's work in light of God's gifting, Christian theology has often used the term *calling*. I, however, prefer the term *responding*, since it serves as a reciprocal counterpart to the fact of God's gifting. Indeed, calling may better be equated with gifting, for the call consists precisely in the fact of having been gifted.

ness, this text asserts that we are created by God; are created as sexual beings, but in such a manner that an individual embodies only one-half of sexual humanity;[3] and are created to responsibly use and develop the rest of the created order. Individually and together these assertions indicate that by divine design personhood consists of relatedness with God, others, and the world in which we live.

If relatedness holds the key to understanding our selves as persons, then we can never answer the question of who we are apart from these relational constraints. Instead, we must know our selves as creature, not Creator, and as the intentional creation brought into being by another's will, not as random and accidental. Thus, our existence declares that we are distinct from God, while also intrinsically linked to God. Similarly, we need to understand our sexual embodiment as a valid, though incomplete, expression of humanity. According to the biblical creation account, our sexuality confronts us with the reality that we live in complementarity. We are always separate from the opposite sex; at the same time we are driven to seek connection with a divinely intended counterpart precisely in the sexual aspect of our being.[4] And finally, to correctly understand our selves from a biblical perspective, we must acknowledge that as human beings we possess Creator-like capacities and traits that set us apart from—actually over—the rest of the world in which we live, even though we fully participate in the "materialness" of all that surrounds and sustains us. Each of the three aspects of the biblical account of the creation of humankind maintains the distinct-but-connected dynamic as central to personhood. Thus, not only does psychology support the notion that identity comes from being in relationship, from experiencing separateness and belonging, but so does a theology that embraces the creation of persons in the image of God.

It is significant that within the theologically crafted account of humanity's creation, the central identity statement of being

3. The pronouncement of being in the image of God falls upon humanity as male and female together (Gen. 1:27).

4. The core quality of sexuality for personhood is especially developed in the theme of Genesis 2 in which the aloneness of the man is characterized as "not good" (v. 18 RSV) and finds divine corrective in the creation of the salvific woman (v. 22), who is gratefully celebrated in the poetic "bone of my bones and flesh of my flesh" paean (v. 23 RSV).

in the image of God is linked so closely with intimacy issues (the male-female relationship and communion with God), industry issues (the mandate to be fruitful, multiply, and subdue and replenish the earth), and integrity issues (the ill-begotten quest for wholeness as expressed in wanting to be like God and grasping for the knowledge of good and evil). Indeed, in the chapters and books that follow Genesis 3, these existential issues appear again and again in the unfolding narratives of alienation and redemption. After all, what are sin and salvation about if not about God-designed selfhood lost and regained, God-ordained intimacy broken and repaired, God-given privileges and God-given mandates abandoned and reacknowledged, and God-intended wholeness destroyed and restored?

Incarnation

The word *intimacy* is not a biblical word. The concept, however, of sharing self and being close is a basic theme in Scripture. In fact, it is possible to view the Bible as an extensive account of God's repeated attempts to disclose the divine self and to be close, that is, be intimate. From the perspective of Christian theology, at the heart of this revelatory activity of God stands the incarnation. Indeed, *incarnation* (embodiment) is the Bible's synonym for intimacy.

For the Christian, God is known best in Jesus Christ. In him God accomplishes the sharing of the divine self, which is variously expressed in such biblical phrases and images as "'Emmanu-el,' (which means, God with us)" (Matt. 1:23 RSV); "the Word was God. . . . And the word became flesh and dwelt among us" (John 1:1, 14 RSV); and "in Him [Christ] dwells all the fullness of the Godhead bodily" (Col. 2:9 NKJV). Or, in less ontological and more relational language, the desire of God to be close to humankind is reduced to the assertion that "God is love," with the incarnation seen as the ultimate expression of that love.

But God's love, God's sharing the divine self with humankind most fully by coming into our midst in Jesus Christ, has a goal. In Christian theology, the love of God for persons becomes the basis for our love of God and neighbor. Hence, Jesus taught that even as God loved him, so he loved his disciples, and so we are to love each other. God's love—God's decision to be intimate with us by living and dying in our midst in the person of Jesus Christ—therefore functions both as empowerment for, and as a model of, intimacy. The New Testament repeatedly grounds calls for intimate behavior on the part of God's people in God's own intimate sharing of self in the incarnation; for example, Saint John wrote:

> And God showed his love for us by sending his only Son into the world, so that we might have life through him. This is what love is: it is not that we have loved God, but that he loved us and sent his Son to be the means by which our sins are forgiven.
> Dear friends, if this is how God loved us, then we should love one another. (1 John 4:9–11 TEV).

A similar emphasis and connection appear in the Epistle to the Ephesians. The instructions in chapters 4 and 5 about proper personal and interpersonal behavior (including familial relationships) are clearly linked to the pivotal reminder that the Christian's own intimate relationship with God derives from the love and self-sharing behavior of the incarnate Christ: "Be kind and tenderhearted to one another, and forgive one another, as God has forgiven you through Christ. Since you are God's dear children, you must try to be like him. Your life must be controlled by love, just as Christ loved us and gave his life for us as a sweet-smelling offering and sacrifice that pleases God" (Eph. 4:32–5:2 TEV).

Theologically conceived, therefore, the task of learning to be intimate—of sharing self with others and letting others share themselves in turn—stands at the heart of personhood. It is modeled by a personal God who shares the divine self with humanity in the incarnation, thereby providing both the paradigm and the power for intimacy on the part of those created in the image of God. Obviously, theology has no less interest in intimacy than does psychology.

Redemption

In classical Christian theology the doctrine of redemption is sometimes referred to as "the work of redemption" (Berkhof 1941, 413ff.). The use of the word *work*, of course, connects this concept with the relational life task of industry. Often, however, the work of redemption is equated with the purpose and activity of God in saving creation from the destructive consequences of sin. Since the redemptive work of Jesus Christ occupies the central role in this divine agenda, and since humanity does not earn salvation by works, it might appear that the work of redemption has no human component. But there are theological and biblical grounds on which to challenge such a conclusion.

Denying a human component in the work of redemption essentially reduces redemption to salvation *from* sin. Though a Christian view must include this aspect, it cannot content itself with this aspect alone since Scripture makes clear that salvation *from* has as its intended goal salvation *for* something. This dual thrust of redemption finds particularly clear expression in Ephesians 2:1–10, which begins with "and you He made alive, who were dead in trespasses and sins" and ends with "for we are His workmanship, created in Christ Jesus for good works, which God prepared beforehand that we should walk in them" (NKJV). This last verse makes it abundantly clear that redemption should eventuate in good works on the part of those who constitute the new creation in Christ.

Particularly because of Protestantism's strong emphasis on salvation by grace through faith, there has been little room in many Christian circles for a theology of "good works," unless it be the good work of the ministry.[5] But what justifies such a narrow understanding of valid work? A narrow understanding of redemption! However, when the redemptive activity of God is understood to include not only the restoration but also the *bringing to completion* of all that God created, a more adequate theology of work emerges. Such a view of work more fully corresponds to the mandate given to man and woman when God first created them; namely, "Have many children, so that your descendants will live all over the earth and bring it under their control. I am putting you in charge . . ." (Gen. 1:28 TEV). Such a view of work also corresponds more adequately to the way that God made human beings, that is, as wondrously creative, gifted, and industrious persons. Indeed, the mandate to subdue and replenish the earth is appropriate precisely because God has

---

5. In this case, blessed are those involved in "full-time ministry" (the clergy) and somewhat less blessed are those others whose daily work is legitimated to the extent that they can witness to others while on the job (the laity).

endowed us with the need and the abilities to do the task in its ever-unfolding variety and complexity.

Work and redemption are not antithetical, nor even simply parallel. Instead, work—the investing of our selves with our unique interests and abilities (gifts)—becomes a way that we can participate in the redemptive agenda of God "to bring all creation together, everything in heaven and on earth, with Christ as head" (Eph. 1:10 TEV). Thus, whether we preach or paint, evangelize or engineer (to the extent that our work represents faithful stewardship of our talents), it is redemptive work.[6] And work undertaken from this perspective enables us to gain identity, share our selves with others, and express our spiritual connection with God.

Kingdom of God

When Jesus taught his disciples how to pray, he urged them to include in their praying the request that God's kingdom come and God's will be done on earth as it is in heaven (Matt. 6:10). Although Christian theology offers no single understanding of the kingdom of God, it seems that Jesus' use of the term in the context of his instruction about prayer links the kingdom of God with a state of affairs in which there is compliance with God's will, or rule. Such an expression of the kingdom embodies an eschatological hope, as expressed in the hymn in Philippians: "And so, in honor of the name of Jesus all beings in heaven, on earth, and in the world below will fall on their knees, and all will openly proclaim that Jesus Christ is Lord, to the glory of God the Father" (2:10–11 TEV). Although this formulation captures the Christian hope of the ultimate and universal realization of the kingdom, in essence it differs little from the present and personal expression of spirituality in the Christian. Thus, both current and future participation in the kingdom of God consists of acknowledging God's absolute claim to sovereignty.

Practically, the kingdom of God comes as we exercise a deep faith that believes wholeness and meaning in life come ultimately from relatedness with God through Christ. It comes as we accept that God is our Creator and recognize the liability (finitude) as well as the responsibility and potential (being in

---

6. Parenting falls under the rubric of work as it is understood here.

the image of God) that pertain to our creatureliness. God's kingdom draws nigh in our embracing of the commandment to love others (both God and neighbor) through sharing our selves, that is, by doing unto them as God has already done unto us. And the rule of God on earth finds expression as we invest our selves in works that are good simply because they contribute to achieving the agenda of God for the creation, namely, "that creation itself would one day be set free from its slavery to decay and would share the glorious freedom of the children of God" (Rom. 8:21 TEV).

The kingdom of God, as defined herein, came to full expression in the person of Jesus. Perhaps it should come as no surprise, then, that when humanistic psychology defines personal wholeness and the self-actualized person (Maslow 1954, 1964), the definitions appear singularly appropriate for a spiritual person such as Jesus. Yet it is precisely because of his spirituality that he stands as a paragon of personal wholeness. Any explanations for Jesus' person, whether psychological or theological, that ignore his spiritual dimension are inadequate. They fail to appreciate the truth that personhood is incomplete without a spiritual component. The quest for wholeness via a relationship with God is an essential relational life task, and one that is recognized by theology and psychology alike.

Application of the RLT Model

What therapeutic use can be made of this paradigm for understanding persons and personal behavior (the RLT model)? Awareness of the categories of the four relational life tasks can aid the therapist or pastor in listening to clients or parishioners talk about problems and areas of pain and growth in their lives. The therapist may be able, because the various tasks are so intertwined, to view a presenting complaint in one area in terms of its relationship to the other three areas. Viewing the complaint in relationship to the whole may facilitate both diagnosis and intervention.

The RLT model can help clients conceptualize issues that concern them. Sometimes the therapist has only to enumerate the four areas of personal development, and the client is able to identify more precisely the task that needs attention. More often, however, clients find it helpful to be made aware of the interconnectedness of the growth tasks in their lives because often they themselves have not seen the connections. For example, a person might not see the relationship between having unclear boundaries of the self and having ongoing difficulty in experiencing intimacy.

One of the most fruitful uses of the RLT model comes in helping people deal with the matter of selfhood. Especially for Christians who have grown up in family and church contexts in which *self* automatically means *selfish*, the notion of gaining self is particularly foreign. For many of these people, sharing self and investing self are theoretically and theologically good, although often emotionally impossible since no sense of self exists. Helping such individuals begin to see the difference between being selfish, being selfless, and having a self—and anchoring these distinctions in theological and psychological reality—is facilitated by use of the RLT model.

Another interesting application of the model comes in relating the relational life tasks to sex roles, and especially doing so within the context of marital counseling. One of the most common issues in marital therapy is the way the partners "miss" each other. A wife, for example, will complain that her husband doesn't talk to her, that he spends all his time on the job, and that she no longer knows who he is. His behavior has left her wondering whether he still loves her and values their relationship and their family life. The husband, on the other hand, can hardly believe that his wife could even ask such a question, and frequently he counters with an incredulous, "For whom do you think I put in all those long hours, if not for you and the kids?" Quite clearly what is going on in a situation like this is confusion about the issues of intimacy and industry, with confusion about aspects of identity and integrity mixed in.

The wife, in sex-stereotypic fashion, has focused her life on intimacy issues. She sees her life revolving around activities of sharing self—giving of her self in nurturing roles, being there for the needs of her family, often acting as the relational hub of the home. Spousing and mothering are not things she *does*; rather, being wife and mother is who she *is*. And what she expects in this role is that her husband will share his person (his identity) with her. But the husband, true to the sex-stereotype of males, has confused his identity with his industry. He also does not *do* carpentry as his work; instead, he *is* a carpenter. And in being a good carpenter, he believes that he is being a good husband. Moreover, he often does not understand what else his wife wants to know about him, for he is hardly aware that there is much more to him than his work. Even when husband and wife are religiously devout persons, their spirituality may not transcend these sex-stereotypic patterns. In some cases, their faith traditions even perpetuate these narrow roles for each of them.

When I work with couples who complain of "missing" each other, I explain the relational life tasks and then ask each to reflect upon how they both are doing with the various tasks. A technique that facilitates this reflection is to have both persons imagine that they each possess 12 chips, which represent their personal resources (time, energy, money, and so on). Their task is to distribute these chips among the four tasks of the model in a manner consistent with the way each actually uses these resources in his or her daily life. When individuals, and couples, do this, they inevitably see an imbalance in their own commitments to being whole persons as well as better understand the imbalances that often exist between them as partners and that contribute to the alienating feelings of isolation or being taken for granted. Women typically see their chips clustered on intimacy, while most men, if they are honest, find theirs piled up on the industry part of the model. Intentional commitment to the relational life task of gaining self often gets no more than 1 chip, and even among persons who define themselves as people of faith, the deliberate pursuit of wholeness through the nurturing of spirituality receives decidedly fewer chips than they would wish to be the case.

A final thought concerning the application of the RLT model pertains to its potential contribution to the challenge of integrating psychology and theology. A case has been made here for the psychological and theological validity of the four relational life tasks and their essential role in being and becoming a person. Since achieving mature personhood is ultimately life's most demanding and worthwhile endeavor, those who work toward the goal deserve access to all the resources that contribute to its attainment, so do those who seek to help others with the process. I dare to hope, therefore, that this particular development and interfacing of the issues of identity, intimacy, industry, and integrity will augment the conceptual and practical repertoire of those committed to bringing both psychological and theological truth to bear upon the process of personal growth.

References

Becker, E. 1973. *The denial of death*. New York: Free Press.

Berkhof, L. 1941. *Systematic theology*. Grand Rapids: Eerdmans.

Boszormenyi-Nagy, I., and G. M. Spark. 1973. *Invisible loyalties: Reciprocity in intergenerational family therapy*. Hagerstown, Md.: Harper and Row.

Bowen, M. 1978. *Family therapy in clinical practice*. New York: Aronson.

Carter, E., and M. McGoldrick. 1980. *The family life cycle: A framework for family therapy*. New York: Gardner Press.

De Koster, L. 1982. *Work, the meaning of your life: A Christian perspective*. Grand Rapids: Christian's Library Press.

Erikson, E. 1950. *Childhood and society*. New York: Norton.

———. 1980. *Identity and the life cycle*. New York: Norton.

Foster, R. 1978. *Celebration of discipline: The path to spiritual growth*. New York: Harper and Row.

Levinson, D. 1978. *The seasons of a man's life*. New York: Knopf.

Luft, J. 1969. *Of human interaction*. Palo Alto, Calif.: National Press Books.

Marks, S. 1986. *Three corners: Exploring marriage and the self*. Lexington, Mass.: Lexington Books.

Maslow, A. 1954. *Motivation and personality*. New York: Harper and Row.

———. 1964. *Religion, values, and peak-experiences*. New York: Viking.

Minuchin, S. 1974. *Families and family therapy*. Cambridge: Harvard University Press.

Raines, J., and D. Day-Lower. 1986. *Modern work and human meaning*. Philadelphia: Westminster.

St. Clair, M. 1986. *Object relations and self psychology*. Monterey, Calif.: Brooks-Cole.

Satir, V. 1972. *Peoplemaking*. Palo Alto, Calif.: Science and Behavior.

Schaefer, M., and D. Olson. 1981. Addressing intimacy: The PAIR inventory. *Journal of Marital and Family Therapy* 7:47–60.

Schaff, P. 1977. *The creeds of Christendom,* vol. 3. Grand Rapids: Baker.

Wynne, L., and A. Wynne. 1986. The quest for intimacy. *Journal of Marital and Family Therapy* 12:383–94.

The Church as a Multigenerational Relational System

Clarence Hibbs

After many years as a Christian, a teacher, and a practitioner of family therapy, I have become increasingly aware that in many ways the behavior of local congregations is like that of families. For some time now, I have been interested in applying theoretical ideas that have proven useful in working with families to interactions within the local church (Hibbs 1983). In this chapter, using the contextual theory developed by Ivan Boszormenyi-Nagy and his associates (Boszormenyi-Nagy and Krasner 1986; Boszormenyi-Nagy and Spark 1973; Boszormenyi-Nagy and Ulrich 1981), I explore the concept of the church as a larger human system, specifically viewing the local congregation as a multigenerational system which develops many of the same kinds of interactional rules, boundaries, and relational functions as families do.

Assuming a systemic, contextual perspective for describing the life of a congregation is in conflict with modern thinking about human interaction, which is primarily individualistic. In contemporary American culture, humans are usually understood as discrete, separate entities (Benjamin 1982, 35). This is a view of human nature largely inherited from a Western, and more specifically Greek, way of thinking which considers the concept of the individual as sacrosanct and absolute (Stein 1985), especially as seen in the philosophy of Nietzsche (Boszormenyi-Nagy and Krasner 1986). This absorption with the self has characterized scholars and the populace alike, and even dominant approaches to psychology support this cultural norm (Wallach and Wallach 1983). One has only to browse through the psychology section of a bookstore and see the titles of self-help books to understand the extent of our culture's preoccupation with the self.

Christianity, unfortunately, has not escaped cultural individualism. Some approaches to the Christian life emphasize an individual's relationship to Christ to the exclusion of his or her relationship to the church. "I can be a Christian without being a member of any church" is an often-heard statement that reflects these approaches. Nothing could be farther from the message of the New Testament (1 Cor. 12:12). Ivan Boszormenyi-Nagy and Barbara Krasner (1986) make the point that family relationships ensue from an ontological fact. Family members are in a relationship by birth; therefore, the relationship has significance from *being* itself. Relatedness in the church is of the same order. Christians are related to each other by reason of birth into Christ. It is not an option whether or not to be related. Relatedness is conferred by baptism into Christ (Gal. 3:26–28). Consequently, the Christian life is seen in the connectedness of people, both with Christ and other Christians.

Changing the focus from separateness to relatedness necessitates a shift in assumptions about humanity (McFarland 1986). Systems theory, the starting point, views the value of the individual in the context of all social relationships. This perspective is more congruent with biblical teaching than 20th-century American individualistic approaches are. Systems theory has been applied to disciplines from physics to history, but only a few applications have been made to larger social systems such as business (Lilienfeld 1978; McFarland 1986; Miller 1973). In the field of family therapy, larger systems have been examined (Imber-Black 1988; Wynne, McDaniel, and Weber 1986), but the only effort to apply family theory to the religious context has been made by Rabbi Edwin H. Friedman (1984, 1985), who examined the interaction of church and synagogue from the Bowenian perspective.

In applying contextual therapy theory to the church, I concentrate in particular on the local church, or congregation. The congregational context has been chosen for two reasons. First, the local church is the most important extended social system, with the possible exception of the extended family, for many people; for some, the congregation supersedes the extended family. Second, I have limited knowledge of churches in which the denominational structure helps form the identity of the church to which one belongs, for my own tradition, the Church of Christ, has no such structure. Moreover, there is evidence that, in practical terms, churches with and without denominational structures are no different in the way the local governance structures shape congregational interaction. For instance, in churches in which the minister, pastor, or priest is seen as the primary person who is in charge, the interactional patterns may be different from churches in which boards of elders, or their equivalent, are seen as the functional leaders who provide the governance. From the multigenerational perspective, the extended denominational identification is roughly equivalent to the extended family and is an important element in the loyalty to a particular local congregation.

Theological Considerations

One feature of my religious tradition is the conviction that any theological position taken should have biblical precedent or justification. Accordingly, as a family therapist and a Christian, I am inclined to find justification for systems theory in the New Testament. However, I undertake this method with caution and will later mention specific difficulties of it. In the writings of the apostle Paul, two metaphors in particular, that of the body and the family, portray the Christian community as an interactional system. These metaphors suggest that each member has an essential and indispensable function to perform for the overall benefit of the church, a concept in harmony with systems theory. Therefore, it seems relevant and useful to integrate biblical teaching and family therapy theory in order to understand the way local congregations function.

The Body

One metaphor with systems implications is the body. This metaphor, which likens the church to the physical body, is found in Romans 12:4–8 and in the more lengthy parallel passage of 1 Corinthians 12:12–31. In these passages, the apostle Paul points out that each part of the body plays an essential role in the health of the whole. To be sure, there are individual functions to be performed, and not all members have the same function, but each part clearly contributes to the whole body. The link between each member is so close that what affects even the smallest one necessarily affects the whole, and it is precisely through the variety of contributions made by individuals that the unity of the church is manifest (Eph. 4:11–16; Banks 1988; Meeks 1983; Minear 1960; Robinson 1952).

The Family

The other metaphor with systems implications, the family, is found in a number of references, again primarily from the apostle Paul. Using the concept of family to describe the congregation suggests that members are, and view one another as, part of a common divine family (Banks 1988).

In Galatians 6:10 RSV and Ephesians 2:19 RSV, the church is called the "household" of God, a term which is roughly equivalent to "family" (Michael 1964–76; Minear 1960). Both passages suggest the familylike relationships found in references that attribute family kinship to Christians. The members are called God's sons and daughters (2 Cor. 6:18), sons through adoption (Gal. 4:4–5), and children and heirs (Rom. 8:14–17). And Christians are given the intimate term "Abba" as a means to address God as Father (Gal. 4:6; Rom. 8:15). Therefore, those who belong see one another as members of a common family (Banks 1988). Paul's favorite description of the relationship between Christians is that of "brethren" (Meeks 1983). Close relationships were evident in the early church; "given the family character of the Christian community, the homes of its members provided the most conducive atmosphere in which they could give expression to the bond they had in common" (Banks 1988, 61).

Modern Theory and Biblical Images

Although it is easy to read into these images the interactive nature of the church, the difficulty of attempting to apply modern theory to them is that one may assume we may mean the same thing by the concepts as did the original writers. This is particularly true with regard to the metaphor of the family. Family forms and structures were no doubt drastically different from our present ones, which in turn brought a very different set of interactional patterns and rules defining family life. This is especially true here, since the primary word used to derive the image of family is the term *household,* which may include many persons besides the nuclear family, such as slaves, freedmen and freedwomen, hired workers, and perhaps tenants and tradesmen (Banks 1988; Meeks 1983; Minear 1960). This difficulty may be present in the work of Martha L. Rogers (1979), who examined the family interactions of several biblical families. In addition, it must not be overlooked that New Testament writers took common terms and concepts and drastically redefined them, giving them unique Christian meaning (Minear 1960).

Further examination of family groups, especially in the New Testament, would be instructive, but is outside the scope of this chapter. It would be intriguing to discover the extent to which families in the early church may have provided the interactional models for congregational interaction.

It seems prudent, then, to take these metaphors in a more general sense, rather than pressing the image to fit the details of a theory. I take the theological connection with theory-making about the church as one in which Scripture presents a picture of the church, especially the local congregation, as an intergenerational social system which recognizes the interdependence of its members with each other. Thus an interactive theory seems closer to the biblical view of the church than an individual-oriented theory.

Theoretical Framework

Although several theoretical approaches could be used to describe a local church as a relational system, the work of Boszormenyi-Nagy and his colleagues (Boszormenyi-Nagy and

Krasner 1986; Boszormenyi-Nagy and Spark 1973; Boszormenyi-Nagy and Ulrich 1981) has been chosen because of its comprehensive scope and its ethical dimension, which is the theory's focus. Boszormenyi-Nagy was deeply influenced by the philosopher Martin Buber (1965), especially by Buber's concept of the I-Thou dialogue, the experiential reciprocity between humans. Boszormenyi-Nagy and Geraldine Spark take particular note of Buber's idea of "the zone of the between," which stimulated the development of the ethical dimension of their theory (1973, 7).

The contextual framework for working with families as expressed by Boszormenyi-Nagy contains four dimensions: objectifiable facts, individual psychology, systems of transactional patterns, and relational ethics (Boszormenyi-Nagy and Krasner 1986; Boszormenyi-Nagy and Ulrich 1981). According to contextual theory, the fourth dimension—relational ethics—encompasses the other three; consequently, the fourth dimension is treated more extensively than the other three. However, the first three dimensions are described here in some detail in an attempt to apply each dimension to the context of the church, since this extension of contextual theory has not been done elsewhere. The following discussion is not intended to be an exhaustive elaboration of Boszormenyi-Nagy's thought, but to stimulate interest in understanding the church as a multigenerational relational system.

Objectifiable Facts

The first dimension consists of objectifiable facts which have to do with preexisting factors and historical facts which have determinative influence on the person or group (Boszormenyi-Nagy and Krasner 1986).

As with any family, a congregation exists in time and space which provide the facts which determine its character and existence. I will use my own tradition to illustrate, and hope that the reader will apply the same principle to his or her background. Although the background of my church has roots in several European religious movements emphasizing a return to the "primitive church" (Allen and Hughes 1988; Hughes and Allen 1988), it is one of the indigenous movements in the United States that arose amid the tumultuous and vigorous expansion following the Revolutionary War (Murch 1962). The restoration movement, as it is called, grew out of a merging of at least four separate groups, each of which sought to throw off the shackles of the past and attempted to restore the primitive nature of the early church. It also had a strong strain of a unity movement, urging Christians to unite under one banner to follow Christ. These paradoxical values have continued in the teaching of the various branches of the restoration movement. The legacy of the ideal of restoration is the stronger among Churches of Christ, one of the three main branches of the movement. The movement's leading mind was Alexander Campbell, who traveled the length and breadth of the westward expansion of the country, preaching and engaging in debates with leading personages from Roman Catholic to atheist positions. Largely through his leadership, a number of theological positions have framed the distinctive nature of Churches of Christ as a religious body. Two issues are of particular importance in shaping the mentality of the movement. The first is the conviction that the local church is autonomous and self-governing. This feature is interesting. Although there is an informal fellowship between congregations, there is no central governing or policy-making body. There is a core of beliefs held in common, but also a wide variation in the specific applications of these beliefs in local churches. The second is the emphasis on restoring the primitive church. The result of this position has been a limited contact with the wider Christian community. It has also had another, more subtle effect. The ideal of attempting to return to the practice of the ancient church has led to a disdain for, if not rejection of, church history.

Consequently, there has been little interest in the historical connections with earlier religious movements or previous theological thought (Allen and Hughes 1988). This amounts to ignoring "facts" contributing to our identity. Nevertheless, these characteristics have made an indelible stamp both on the way congregations interact with the wider community and how internal relationships within the local churches operate. Thus, the local church operates in its own time, anchored only in the primitive church.

The local church is also situated in space. The geographical location of a congregation determines much about its makeup. Churches of Christ have been more numerous in the South and

Southwest, and, until recently, have been more rural than urban. The cultural climate of congregations in other locations often reflect these origins. During the Great Depression numerous people moved from the Southwest to central California; among them were many members of the Churches of Christ. In many ways, the congregations of these members' descendants are more like the churches in Oklahoma, Arkansas, and Texas than like the surrounding California culture.

Also contributing to the character of a church are events and experiences that are beyond its control. A large congregation with which I worked for a number of years was actually the product of a congregation that had moved from the central part of the city to the suburbs. Although a large remnant of the membership from the downtown church remained, the majority of members came from the suburbs, thus changing the character of the congregation drastically. No longer composed of older, less-affluent members, the church was made up of younger, middle-class parishioners. The mood or emotional climate of the congregation changed from pessimism to optimism, resulting in the expansion of programs and activities. Having faced the dilemma of a declining membership by moving to a more promising location, the church avoided its own demise. Such change is not always an option, however. Some rural and small-town congregations faced with changing economic and demographic conditions witness the slow decay and disappearance of their communities, ceasing to exist themselves like childless families who cease to exist when the spouses die.

Conflict, especially a rift that exists over a long period of time, also affects the character of a church. If the rift is covert, then overt conflicts will likely break out along the covert lines of disagreement, as happens in families. However, overt conflicts will likely be over issues more acceptable than the covert ones, such as doctrine. This kind of displacement is a well-known phenomenon for family therapists, who observe families fighting over issues which are only symptoms of the basic schism within the family system. A good example of such displacement in a congregation is found in a church that grew over many years because of the principal leadership of two families. Over time, conflicts developed, but they were not negotiated and healed. Consequently, a covert division prevailed for several years; indeed, the ghosts of the original families continued to influence decisions and policies, perhaps as did the legacy of the legendary Hatfields and McCoys in American folklore. When a new minister was called to serve the congregation, the invisible loyalties of the previous generations persisted. Whether a parishioner was satisfied with or opposed to the newcomer's ministry largely followed old lines of disagreement, thus following structural rules that were oblivious to the participants and quite apart from the real issues.

In contrast, open communication and free negotiation characterized the previously mentioned congregation that had moved from the city to the suburbs. Members of this congregation held a diversity of viewpoints over a wide spectrum of issues. The church's ability to adjust to new conditions provided the climate in which problems were solved creatively, in much the same way a "healthy" family functions (Beavers 1982, 45–66).

The cited examples—history, location, outside factors, and conflicts—demonstrate that the objectifiable facts of a congregation's intergenerational and contextual history have important determinitive effects on the way a congregation interacts. If these facts are not recognized or are ignored, much about a congregation's present functioning may be misunderstood.

Individual Psychology

With relation to contextual family theory, individual psychology, the second dimension, denotes the makeup of each individual in a family (Boszormenyi-Nagy and Krasner 1986). Applied to a congregation, individual psychology refers to the makeup of each member. The complexity of this dimension relates proportionally (maybe exponentially) to the number of members. An individual has characteristics that have been shaped by his or her genetic makeup, past experiences, level of intelligence, emotional predisposition, needs, goals, and motivations. In a large group, possibilities exist for all kinds of positive as well as negative interpersonal situations. The personal tastes of one individual may be repugnant to another. The past experience of one person may have fostered a cynicism which another individual cannot understand. One member with a rural background may prefer simple, informal, and straightforward forms of worship, while another with an urban heritage might crave a more formal and sophisticated service.

That individual members have their own family histories complicates this dimension. In fact, it is useful to view families as individual units within the church. Each family brings its own rules and patterns of interaction, which have to be meshed in the larger system of the congregation. Sorting out the effect of individual and familial psychologies is a particular challenge to any congregation that is culturally heterogeneous. One minister recently described his church as a "little United Nations," a characterization prompted by several incidents that revealed the difficulty people of diverse backgrounds had in understanding each other and working together.

Systems of Transactional Patterns

The third dimension of contextual therapy concerns the systems of transactional patterns present in family interaction, which contextual therapists use as part, though not the most crucial part, of the total context of therapy (Boszormenyi-Nagy and Krasner 1986). In this they differ from most other family therapies, which focus intensively on this dimension. The basic principle is that elements in a system are regulated in the way they change or stay the same (Schultz 1984). Within a system, morphostasis (the homeostatic force) and morphogenesis (the accommodative force) tend to keep the system within a prescribed range of behavior (Becvar and Becvar 1988; Hoffman 1981).

Systemic concepts can be used to understand a church's behavior regarding specific elements of congregational life. For example, a religious tradition that allows a certain flexibility in the conducting of worship services would react if experimenting went beyond the specified bounds. In some communions, the personal behavior of members is prescribed, and the regulation of behavior may be formal and overt or covert. Consider a congregation's stance on divorce. If strictures against divorce are strong, then a church will apply pressure to keep a member from obtaining one. In the event that the divorce is obtained, the member could face consequences such as excommunication, shunning, or forbiddance of remarriage.

A human system, whether it be a family or congregation, can be classified as either open or closed. The classification is based on the way information is permitted to flow in and out of the system as well as on the amount of contact with the outside world allowed its members (Becvar and Becvar 1982). In a congregation, the method of assimilating new members and families reflects the type of system under which the group operates. An expanding, open congregation seeks and welcomes new members, acts which demonstrate morphogenesis. A less flexible, closed congregation treats new members as outsiders, which demonstrates morphostasis.

Attitudes toward doctrinal statements or beliefs can also reflect the homeostatic or accommodative forces of a congregation. Whether there has been a long-standing informal tradition or formalized creeds and theologies, deviations away from the norm are likely to be greeted with resistance or alarm. What might happen when the role of women in the structure and worship of a church is examined? If a change in policies regarding women's participation is proposed, it may be interpreted as antibiblical or as a threat to the existing hierarchy. A negative reaction would likely be strong as various forces strive to maintain the status quo.

Rules and boundaries within a congregational system may affect the interaction of members more than the doctrinal formulations. Creedal statements, church regulations, and traditions illustrate boundary markers, such as who is a church member and who is not and which beliefs are required or which are permitted. However, within the group there are idiosyncratic relationship patterns, roles, and rules that distinguish it as an interactional system. For instance, rules about who participates and in what way are revealed in these covert patterns, which at first are as invisible to the outsider as those of a family to the naive viewer (Becvar and Becvar 1988). Such rules determine how members approach church officials with complaints or problems, for example. One person may be more approachable or accessible than others. Moreover, it might be acceptable to broach only a limited range of issues, while others are covertly defined as taboo. Perhaps an approach to the minister or pastor can be made only through established procedures not spelled out but understood by the group.

The organizational structure of any church helps define how interaction takes place within the congregation. Most systems can be characterized as having a hierarchy (Becvar and Becvar 1988). In a congregational system, both an internal and external hierarchy affect the behavior of those inside the local congregation. In most churches the minister, pastor, or priest is the person in charge. In many free church traditions, a board of parishioners (known variously as the elders, presbyters, stewards, or vestry) sets policy within which the role of the minister as well as other members is defined. In other churches, denominational entities such as synods, dioceses, and presbyteries provide structure, which shapes the character of the interaction within individual congregations. These hierarchical differences alter the character of the rules and interactive patterns of the group.

Natural subsystems are found in any church group in the same way they are in a family (Minuchin 1974). Some subsystems are established consciously for organizational purposes (e.g., the elders and deacons) or for specific tasks (e.g., bazaar or building-project committee). Other subsystems spring up informally because of the members' ages or interests (e.g., youth groups, singles, or seniors). To the extent that these subsystems remain flexible and are able to adapt to changing circumstances, they will be a healthy part of the group. When subsystems become rigid and inflexible, they begin to make interaction difficult.

An important aspect of family life is the way provision is made for the growth of family members. From an object-relations perspective, Cameron Lee (1985) describes the "good-enough" family as one that provides a proper relational context in which the self can grow amid the challenges of life and is able to tolerate without fragmentation the inherent ambiguities of existence. From the Christian viewpoint, he describes this family as a "community of grace" in which each person is secure, participates and contributes to the needs of others, and is able to form bilateral commitments outside the family. Considering another system, Lee wonders about the implication of the good-enough family for the family of God. His description suggests that if the concept were applied to the church, the atmosphere surrounding the congregation would be conducive not only to psychological and physical growth but also to spiritual growth. As in families, such an atmosphere ordinarily takes much careful effort and planning. In such a supportive and accepting context, the spiritual community of grace can grow and mature, and reach into the wider community as well.

It is important to note that although the second and third dimensions might be construed as discrete from each other, this is not the case in contextual theory. In fact, all dimensions are seen to intersect and interact at many points (Boszormenyi-Nagy and Krasner 1986). James Framo (1981) sees the relationship between the individual dimension and the transactional or systemic dimension as essential for understanding of how each individual is developed and shaped by the interaction with self, family, and other larger systems. Either dimension alone offers an inadequate explanation of human behavior. Contextual theory integrates and expands these dimensions through a fourth dimension.

Relational Ethics

The fourth dimension of contextual family therapy is relational ethics, which is assumed to encompass and transcend the other three dimensions (Boszormenyi-Nagy 1987; Boszormenyi-Nagy and Krasner 1986). Relational ethics, as contextual theory uses the term, does not have specific moral content, but rather "is concerned with a balance of equitable fairness between people. . . . We consider relational ethics to be a fundamental dynamic force, holding family and societal relationships together through mutuality and trustworthiness of relationship" (Boszormenyi-Nagy and Ulrich 1981, 160). The emphasis, then, is on "responsibility for the relational consequences" and results in the validation and benefit of all parties in relationships (Boszormenyi-Nagy 1987, 296).

Basis of Relational Ethics. Contextual theorists view relational ethics as "a fundamental dynamic force." Since the force is presumably innate or natural, theorists, such as Boszormenyi-Nagy (1988), simply assume the concept to be true. For Christians, however, a crucial element is missing from the formulation: a standard. If there is no standard to which the values of fairness, justice, and trust must plead, it would appear that social convention or preference would be the reasons for choosing them. For Christians, the grounds for one person to expect fair treatment, or justice, or for one to act in the best interest of another is not a human invention, but is the love of God, who first acted in our best interest (1 John 4:7–12, 19; Krone 1983; Lewis 1943).

Without the standard of God's love (see Stauffer 1964–76, 44–54, for an examination of the biblical use of love), there is no intrinsic reason why one should adopt the values of fairness, justice, and trust. But God first acted in our ultimate best interest and bids us, even requires us, to follow that example. By giving freely, God, the perfect example, set the standard of trustworthiness, justice, and fairness to follow. Our biblical motivation for fairness and the just treatment of fellow human beings is that we are the recipients of God's grace and justification through forgiveness. Thus, God's action is the standard for what Boszormenyi-Nagy calls the ethical dimension in human relationships. In order for Christians to accept the concept, it seems necessary to add the standard of God's love as the basis of Boszormenyi-Nagy's formulation of relational ethics. God's actions of love and care are the basis of the Christian's behavior.

Justice, or Fairness. The contextual concept of justice is relational rather than judicial. It is a "principle of equity of mutual give-and-take which guides the individual member of a social group in facing the ultimate consequences of his [or her] relationship with others" (Boszormenyi-Nagy and Spark 1973, 61). Also, in the world of human relationships, there is a constant oscillation between obligations and fulfilment of obligations, in which one day's balance becomes tomorrow's imbalance.

In the context of a congregation, members have the same need for relational justice as do members of a family. Relationships within a congregation may be seen as a spiritual give-and-take in which members recognize the mutual obligations of both giving and receiving, for balance in relationships implies willingness to receive as well as to take. If the balance of fairness is maintained, parishioners receive justice by virtue of their membership. Consider, for example, what is taught in 1 Corinthians through the metaphor of the body: "the members . . . have the same care for one another. If one member suffers, all suffer together; if one member is honored, all rejoice together" (12:25b–26 RSV).

In the well-functioning congregation, the roles of the various individuals contribute to the overall care, and when injustices are noticed, steps are taken to correct them (Boszormenyi-Nagy and Ulrich 1981). Also, the talents or abilities of an individual or group contribute to the well-being of the congregation so that the whole is served (Rom. 12:4–8). Fairness, however, is not absolute. There is an inherent asymmetry in human relationships (e.g., the difference between parent and child), and the give-and-take depends on each person's capacity for giving as well as taking (van Heusden and van den Eerenbeemt 1987). Quite possibly many disputes in congregations have been triggered by an imbalance of fairness. As coalitions of individuals or groups form around an issue, the issue itself may be covering invisible loyalties. For instance, one congregation was split seemingly along the lines of supporting and opposing the youth minister, who was criticized for unwise behavior. However, the groups were formed more closely along the lines of the "old-timers" and "newcomers," who were both concerned whether their level of influence in congregational decision making was fair.

Multigenerational Context. The relational context of a system is multigenerational, including at least three generations. The psychological and ethical meanings are lost if they are not seen in a relational, multigenerational perspective (Boszormenyi-Nagy and Ulrich 1981). As a family does, a congregation over time develops transactional patterns, rules, and behaviors, which changes in membership and leadership may not alter. Also, as in a family, the particular way in which a congregation carries out a function may be the product of traditions established by its members several generations back.

A congregation's multigenerational context is readily seen in the example of a church that had existed about 25 years. A core of members had been in the church since the congregation began. As the church grew, new members suggested that the buildings and grounds be refurbished in a certain way. Resistance to the changes was expressed with the fear that it "would hurt the feelings of those who had worked so hard to build this church." Other cosmetic-type changes may have multigenerational implications as well. For example, theologically unimportant customs about how worship services are conducted commonly cause concern. In one congregation the printing of an order of worship was interpreted as departing from "the way it has always been done," implying that to add this element would be disloyal to those of the past who felt no need for such structure.

Multigenerational interactional patterns in a congregation often follow informal, rather than direct, lines of communication, much as they do in a family. The patterns may prescribe who is sought for advice, who relays messages to church leaders, and how functions are carried out. The rationale for these preferred ways of interacting may escape outside observers unless they are aware the patterns are the result of lengthy development over time.

Trust and Trustworthiness. Out of the concept of justice, the concept of trust and trustworthiness has been developed in contextual theory (van Heusden and van den Eerenbeemt 1987). The capacity for balancing the consequences of one's having benefited from another's care and the obligation to offer due consideration in return is relational justice and leads to interpersonal trust (Boszormenyi-Nagy and Krasner 1986). Trustworthiness, then, is the glue of viable relationships, a condition established over a long time by the give-and-take of reliable partners. Trust is necessary for healthy relationships, but those to be trusted must be trustworthy. Therefore, trust is an interpersonal dimension (Karpel and Strauss 1983).

Believing that God is ultimately trustworthy, Christians put their whole trust in God. In turn, this act of trust inspires Christians to risk trustworthiness in their own actions and to trust other people in return. In a context of trust, people are able to act with due regard for the interest of others as well as the self. Throughout Scripture, this model of trust and concern for others, which is based on the actions of God, is held up as a standard for Christian behavior (e.g., Phil. 2:4–8).

There is no realm in which trust and trustworthiness should flourish more than in a congregation. The church teaches that Christians are not to seek an advantage over others, and, within its bounds, one expects others to tell the truth, to carry out their commitments, and even to be openhandedly generous without expecting a return. The church, a community in which trust is the norm, is at odds with the larger culture. Outside the church, whether it be at school or work, one often finds that words other than trust best describe relationships, words such as deception, cheating, and stinginess.

It is in the realm of church relationships that the model of trust and trustworthiness turns the dominant cultural value of self-interest on its head. The dominant culture promotes a climate in which self-concern, self-sufficiency, and self-expression are seen as the ultimate good (Wallach and Wallach 1983). The decisive question from this point of view is "What's in it for me?" In contrast, the Christian value system, which is congruent with contextual concepts of justice and trustworthiness, asserts that the interest of others is as important as the interest of self. If the church takes this seriously, it will find opposition from all quarters.

For Christians, the model of trust and trustworthiness leads to some very practical dilemmas. Consider, for example, what children are taught and what is expected of them regarding strangers. At worship services, there is an atmosphere in which strangers are welcome. Often these strangers speak to or touch small children, and expect to be accepted by them. But in current society, in an effort to protect children from harm, they are taught not to talk to strangers and to refuse to allow others to touch them. How are children to make the distinction between the trusting atmosphere of the church and the dangerous atmosphere outside it? Worse, what if someone from the church community molests a child?

Christians also face a dilemma when church teaching expounds trust and due consideration but the practice of the leadership reveals self-interest and angling for advantage, prestige, and power. For example, simply recall the stories of some well-known televangelists. If reports of their actions are true, the tragedy, at least in part, is that the contradictions between church teaching and practice are ridiculed.

Loyalty. Loyalty, an indispensable concept of relational ethics for Boszormenyi-Nagy and his colleagues, is an internalized set of expectations and a set of specifiable attitudes that comply with internalized injunctions aroused from a sense of duty, fairness, or justice. People behave loyally for various reasons: they are externally coerced; they consciously recognize a feeling of obligation; they feel an unconscious binding obligation to belong. Both in families and larger society, loyalty has strong fibers that hold together complex pieces of relationships (Boszormenyi-Nagy and Spark 1973).

In the Old Testament, the concept of loyalty is best expressed by the Hebrew word *hesed*, which is often translated as "steadfast love" (Krone 1983). It is unlikely that loyalty is a human invention. Rather, it is the loyalty of God, which is manifest in God's actions toward humankind, that is the basis of human loyalty. Therefore, the loyalty of God becomes the model for human actions of loyalty. Boszormenyi-Nagy comes close to this theological concept but stops short of acknowledging the religious basis. When he argues for the necessity of loyalty, the "existence of structured group expectations to which all members are committed," he credits Buber's idea of the "order of the human world" (Boszormenyi-Nagy and Spark 1973, 37).

Loyalty is both vertical and horizontal. Vertical loyalty exists between generations and is asymmetrical (i.e., the obligation is not equally distributed among generations) in nature. Horizontal loyalty exists in the present generation and is more symmetrical (i.e., the obligation is reciprocal and essentially equal; van Heusden and van den Eerenbeemt 1987). For the Christian, the primary vertical loyalty is to God; however, an internalized vertical loyalty is largely acquired in the context of the community, the church. Therefore, the bond of loyalty is not only a faithfulness to the principles and symbolic definitions of the church, but also a mutual commitment between the people within the congregation (Boszormenyi-Nagy and Spark 1973).

As individuals grow up in the context of the church, they internalize attitudes, relational rules, and conceptions of acceptable and unacceptable behavior, just as they do in their families. As a young person growing up, I was the recipient of the concern and guidance of people who were committed to the Lord. I heard the stories of missionaries and others who had suffered hardship for their faith, and my loyalty was strengthened. I learned to trust through my interactions with and observation of people whose word was reliable. In this way, I learned loyalty to both the principles of Christianity and to the people who made up the church.

As children grow up in a congregation, they usually find themselves in the context of several generations. Their peers, their parents, their grandparents, single people, widows, and widowers are a part of the milieu in which the children talk, play, listen, and worship. As the church traditions are enacted before the children and as the members exhibit care for and interest in them, loyalty bonds form naturally. In this way, the congregation becomes a multigenerational system that is both a source and an object of loyalty. The symbolic meanings are transmitted through worship and teaching, and bonds of loyalty seem to maintain the community (Boszormenyi-Nagy and Spark 1973). In the New Testament, the word for loyalty is translated as "faithfulness." Not surprisingly, the church is described as the community of the faithful (e.g., Eph. 1:1; 1 Tim. 3:11; 2 Tim. 2:2; Rev. 2:10).

Vertical loyalty can be exhibited in yet another way: in faithfulness to the church of one's youth. In our mobile society, it is likely that people will be connected to a number of congregations during their lifetimes. In the free church tradition, it is likely that the practice of worship as well as the character of the congregation will vary widely from place to place, especially where great distances separate them. If one's "invisible loyalties" are to the place where one grew up, there can be a tendency to define any difference from that place as wrong or deviant. Thus, embracing the practices of a different congregation is regarded as disloyal.

Strong loyalty to one's original church is demonstrated in the case of a family who moved to a community from another state, where they had been very involved in their local congregation. The family began to involve themselves aggressively in a new congregation, but quickly found it to have different customs and practices. At first, the differences evoked puzzlement, which was followed by resistance and anger. The family members made constant references to "where we came from," implying that things were done "right" there and "wrong" in the new church. Although these reactions might be common, this family was simply unable to adjust. Another way to understand this family's reaction is to regard it as split loyalty (Boszormenyi-Nagy and Ulrich 1981). Apparently, the family perceived a conflict in which they could not be loyal to their home church and the new one at the same time. To develop horizontal loyalty to the new church would imply acceptance of customs opposed by the old one, and this proved to be too much.

Horizontal loyalties are the rights and obligations that people in their own time undertake mutually and voluntarily (van Heusden and van den Eerenbeemt 1987). Such loyalties affect an important part of the functioning of a congregation: the way it organizes to nurture and care for its members. Parishioners exhibit due care for each other in the normal course of the congregation's life. When members are treated as family, the church community functions as an extended family. For example, an elderly man who had lost his wife was treated as a father or grandfather and interacted with numerous parishioners as if he were a family member. When he was unable to care for himself, members of the church attended him by bringing meals, seeing to his business affairs, and eventually assisting him in finding a suitable care facility. These actions of horizontal loyalty are also transgenerational, in that they translate into "terms of benefit for future generations" (Boszormenyi-Nagy and Krasner 1986, 129).

The issue of loyalty suggests a recognition of two contrasting concepts: indebtedness and guilt. Indebtedness is the realization of what one owes because of the loyal actions of someone else (Karpel and Strauss 1983). One can be indebted at both the vertical and horizontal levels. Many people remain loyal to the denominational ties of their birth as much out of loyalty to those who taught them the gospel as anything else. In addition to invisible loyalty to the family, emotional ties with people who constitute the spiritual family create strong bonds of loyalty that are not easily set aside.

Recognition of indebtedness and positive discharge of the corresponding obligations result in trust. Failing to meet the obligations or turning one's back on them results in the experience of guilt (Boszormenyi-Nagy and Spark 1973). In the professional literature, guilt itself can be either healthy or pathological, existential or neurotic. But developing the capacity for guilt is a significant accomplishment in a person's ability to maintain relationships (Karpel and Strauss 1983). If it were not for the feeling of guilt, many destructive acts would likely be carried out.

At the spiritual level, guilt is the recognition of sin. Sin, as a condition which reflects a ruptured relationship with God, is an act for which no rejunctive (i.e., relationship enhancing) action is possible beyond the atonement already made, thus creating a vertical ledger of indebtedness (Piercy, Sprenkle, and associates 1986). However, one cannot pay God back for wrong inflicted. The sovereign action of God in forgiveness, therefore, does not fit the concept of balancing ledgers, since relational debts can only be paid back to those to whom they are owed (Boszormenyi-Nagy and Ulrich 1981, 160). This "eye for an eye, tooth for a tooth" focus is one of the serious limitations of contextual theory as developed by Boszormenyi-Nagy and his colleagues.

Forgiveness. Though the theological concept of forgiveness is not found in contextual therapy, a related concept—exoneration—is. Boszormenyi-Nagy and Krasner (1986) make a distinction between the two concepts. For them, forgiveness retains the assumption of guilt on the part of the one forgiven, but exoneration is seen as a reassessment of the offender's past in which that person is also seen as a victim.

From the biblical standpoint, the distinction between exoneration and forgiveness cannot be maintained. In Scripture, forgiveness is complete release from sin and does not imply further assumption of guilt (Col. 1:14; 2:13–14; Eph. 1:7; Heb. 10:16–18; Rom. 5:18; Bultmann 1964–76). Atonement is the action of God, which made forgiveness thorough and complete (Rom. 3:21–26). Forgiveness does not involve a reassessment of the past, but instead erases the guilt completely (Col. 2:13–14) and sets the example for Christians to follow (Col. 3:13). Jesus taught forgiveness as an essential part of the Christian life (Matt. 6:12–15; 18:21–22; Krone 1983), with God's unilateral forgiveness as the motivation (Eph. 4:32). For both the offender and the offended, the practical difference between forgiveness and exoneration is indistinguishable. As Hendrika Vande Kemp (1987) points out, forgiveness is a relational act in much the same way that exoneration, as defined by contextual theorists, is. Whether it is God's forgiveness or one person's forgiveness of another, forgiveness is a relational act.

Boszormenyi-Nagy and Krasner (1986) point out the relational benefits of exoneration in improving the present functioning of the family. The benefits come in the form of trustworthy relationships. The one who exonerates, as well as the one who forgives, is able to act with due care toward others without the destructive entitlement previously held.

How might the relational benefits of exoneration, or forgiveness, improve the functioning of the church family? Let's consider a specific issue. Many churches, like many families, have a legacy of racial prejudice of one kind or another. How does the present church address rejunctive action and move forward without continuing the pattern of injustice and unfairness? There must be a call for exoneration or forgiveness. Recognition of the previous victims of prejudice and the sins of previous generations would open the door for exoneration or forgiveness. Thereafter, the present church would be free to act in trustworthiness and fairness to all people, thus exhibiting loyalty to Christ's mandate to love all humankind.

Conclusion

Boszormenyi-Nagy and his colleagues have taken family therapy theory a crucial step forward—beyond individual and systemic concepts to describe relational ethics as the common denominator of human interaction (Boszormenyi-Nagy 1987). The various elements of contextual theory have many points of congruence with Christian teaching (Krone 1983). And contextual theory has much to offer those examining family therapy from a Christian viewpoint. Moreover, since congregations function in much the same way as families, the application of contextual theory to the church can lead to a better understanding of congregational life.

This chapter has been an attempt to apply the four dimensions of contextual theory to a larger social system, the congregation of the Christian church. The first dimension, objectifiable facts, relates to the larger context (in time and space) of a congregation. The second dimension, individual psychology, pertains to the individual makeup of each church member. In a congregation this dimension can be quite complex since individual makeup is shaped not only by genetic and physiological factors, but also by social influences from significant interactions in any area of life as argued by both object relations theorists and interpersonal psychologists. The third dimension, systems of transactional patterns, reveals patterns of interaction that have been developed in a congregation.

Relational ethics, the fourth and most important dimension, supports biblical concepts as they apply to healthy functioning. Fairness, justice, and loyalty, as expounded in contextual theory, demonstrate that biblical teaching is a viable basis for productive and fulfilling lives. These concepts are fundamental aspects of optimal human functioning because they are given by God and are characteristics of God as a relational being. As God's creation, humans function best when they behave in harmony with their maker. Church teaching promotes justice, fairness, and loyalty, and should be the model of these ideals in real life.

Not every concept of contextual theory has been explored in this chapter. However, it is hoped that this attempt will stimulate further refinement and discussion of the integration of useful theory with biblical teaching.

References

Allen, C. L., and R. T. Hughes. 1988. *Discovering our roots: The ancestry of Churches of Christ.* Abilene, Tex.: Abilene Christian University Press.

Banks, R. 1988. *Paul's idea of community.* Grand Rapids: Eerdmans.

Beavers, W. R. 1982. Healthy, midrange, and severely dysfunctional families. In *Normal family processes*, ed. F. Walsh, 45–66. New York: Guilford Press.

Becvar, R. J., and D. S. Becvar. 1982. *Systems theory and family therapy.* Lanham, Md.: University Press of America.

————. 1988. *Family therapy: A systemic integration.* Boston: Allyn.

Benjamin, M. 1982. General systems theory, family systems theories, and family therapy: Towards an integrated model of family process. In *Family therapy: Principles of strategic practice*, ed. A. Bross, 34–88. New York: Guilford Press.

Boszormenyi-Nagy, I. 1987. Transgenerational solidarity: The expanding context of therapy and prevention. In *Foundations of contextual therapy: Collected papers of Ivan Boszormenyi-Nagy, M.D.*, 292–318. New York: Brunner/Mazel.

————. 1988. Roots of freedom: Theory and practice of contextual therapy. Paper presented at the Annual Conference of the American

Association for Marriage and Family Therapy, New Orleans, October.

Boszormenyi-Nagy, I., and B. R. Krasner. 1986. *Between give and take: A clinical guide to contextual therapy*. New York: Brunner/Mazel.

Boszormenyi-Nagy, I., and D. N. Ulrich. 1981. Contextual family therapy. In *Handbook of family therapy*, ed. A. S. Gurman and D. P. Kniskern, 159–86. New York: Brunner/Mazel.

Boszormenyi-Nagy, I., and G. M. Spark. 1973. *Invisible loyalties: Reciprocity in intergenerational family therapy*. Hagerstown, Md.: Harper and Row.

Buber, M. 1965. *The knowledge of man: A philosophy of the interhuman*. Trans. M. Friedman and R. G. Smith. New York: Harper and Row. Original German edition published 1923.

Bultmann, R. 1964–76. Aphiémi. In *Theological dictionary of the New Testament*, ed. G. Kittel, G. Friedrich, and G. W. Bromiley, trans. G. W. Bromiley, 10 vols. Grand Rapids: Eerdmans. 1:509–12.

Framo, J. 1981. The integration of marital therapy with sessions with family of origin. In *Handbook of family therapy*, ed. A. S. Gurman and D. P. Kniskern, 133–58. New York: Brunner/Mazel.

Friedman, E. H. 1984. Churches and synagogues. In *Practicing family therapy in diverse settings*, ed. M. Berger, G. J. Jurkovic, and associates, 271–300. San Francisco: Jossey-Bass.

———. 1985. *Generation to generation: Family process in church and synagogue*. New York: Guilford Press.

van Heusden, A., and E. van den Eerenbeemt. 1987. *Balance in motion: Ivan Boszormenyi-Nagy and his vision of individual and family therapy*. Trans. A. van Heusden, E. van den Eerenbeemt, and I. Boszormenyi-Nagy. New York: Brunner/Mazel. Original Dutch edition published 1983.

Hibbs, C. 1983. A systems theory view of the church. *Journal of Psychology and Christianity* 2:26–30.

Hoffman, L. 1981. *Foundations of family therapy: A conceptual framework of systems change*. New York: Basic.

Hughes, R. T., and C. L. Allen. 1988. *Illusions of innocence: Protestant primitivism in America, 1630–1875*. Chicago: University of Chicago Press.

Imber-Black, E. 1988. *Families and larger systems*. New York: Guilford Press.

Karpel, M. A., and E. S. Strauss. 1983. *Family evaluation*. New York: Gardner Press.

Krone, L. C. 1983. Justice as a relational and theological cornerstone. *Journal of Psychology and Christianity* 2:36–46.

Lee, C. 1985. The good-enough family. *Journal of Psychology and Theology* 13:182–89.

Lewis, C. S. 1943. *Mere Christianity*. New York: Macmillan.

Lilienfield, R. 1978. *The rise of systems theory: An ideological analysis*. New York: Wiley.

McFarland, D. E. 1986. *The managerial imperative*. Cambridge, Mass.: Ballinger Publishing.

Meeks, W. A. 1983. *The first urban Christians*. New Haven: Yale University Press.

Michael, O. 1964–76. Oikos. In *Theological dictionary of the New Testament*, ed. G. Kittel, G. Friedrich, and G. W. Bromiley, trans. G. W. Bromiley, 10 vols. Grand Rapids: Eerdmans. 5:119–34.

Miller, J. G. 1973. The nature of living systems. In *Organizational systems: General systems approaches to complex organizations*, ed. F. Baker, 35–72. Homewood, Ill.: Irwin.

Minear, P. 1960. *Images of the church in the New Testament*. Philadelphia: Westminster.

Minuchin, S. 1974. *Families and family therapy*. Cambridge: Harvard University Press.

Murch, J. D. 1962. *Christians only*. Cincinnati: Standard Publishing.

Piercy, F. P., D. H. Sprenkle, and associates. 1986. *Family therapy sourcebook*. New York: Guilford Press.

Robinson, J. A. T. 1952. *The body: A study in Pauline theology*. London: Student Christian Movement Press.

Rogers, M. L. 1979. Some Bible families examined from a systems perspective. *Journal of Psychology and Theology* 7:251–58.

Schultz, S. J. 1984. *Family systems theory: An integration*. New York: Aronson.

Stauffer, E. 1964–76. Agapaō. In *Theological dictionary of the New Testament*, ed. G. Kittel, G. Friedrich, and G. W. Bromiley, trans. G. W. Bromiley, 10 vols. Grand Rapids: Eerdmans. 1:21–55.

Stein, H. F. 1985. Values and family therapy. In *Families and other systems*, ed. J. Schwartzman, 201–43. New York: Guilford Press.

Vande Kemp, H. 1987. Relational ethics in the novels of Charles Williams. *Family Process* 26:283–94.

Wallach, M. A., and L. Wallach. 1983. *Psychology's sanction for selfishness: The error of egoism in theory and therapy*. San Francisco: W. H. Freeman.

Wynne, L. C., S. H. McDaniel, and T. T. Weber. 1986. *Systems consultation: A new perspective for family therapy.* New York: Guilford Press.

Between Truth and Trust: Elements of Direct Address

Barbara R. Krasner and Austin J. Joyce

Introduction: The Elements of Direct Address

Therapy is about transforming moments. People tell their stories; therapists respond. The stories that are told are always in process. The responses that are given are always affected by the quest for meaning that has shaped a therapist's life. Therapy is about ordinary moments that are preludes to healing ordinary lives. In one form or another, healing occurs through genuinely trustworthy exchange. By accident or design, every legitimate mode of psychotherapy is based on the sacred foundation of trust. Trust is to committed relationship what food is to the sustenance of life, for "what he [the problematic person] wants is a being not only whom he can trust as a person trusts another, but a being that gives him now the certitude that 'there *is* a soil, there *is* an existence. The world is not condemned to deprivation, degeneration, destruction. The world *can* be redeemed. I can be redeemed because there is this trust'" (Buber 1965, 183; Buber's italics). Therapist and client commit themselves to a contract through which to explore and

135

invest in the redeeming options of a trustworthy way. Therapeutic modes are molded and informed by many factors: biology, psychology, family, and culture. Less immediately visible are the philosophical foundations which undergird a therapists's practice and conviction.

This writing was born out of the authors' individual and collective passion for the ethics of direct address. In our journeys toward personal balance and professional maturity and competence, each of us has struggled with the painful consequences of not having been heard. And we live with the regret of having failed to hear a loved one's still, small voice. Each of us has suffered from the limitations of our parents' lives and actions. Each of us has had occasion to stand helplessly by as our contributions to family members have been overlooked and gone uncredited. Each of us has experienced withered self-esteem impaled on the jagged edge of disappointed parental expectations, and each of us has encountered marital, filial, and sibling anticipations and hopes that we have failed to meet. And though this writing is born of struggle, it is also born of joy, for it is inspirited by the courageous, if sometimes unheralded, gifts of our parents' lives and contributions. Each of us has been witness to hidden resources that have arisen out of the breach of injury, estrangement, and mistrust between us and our family members. From time to time each of us has bathed in the deep, pure waters of our families' adulation and basked in the strong, bright light of their nurture, their love, and their care.

Nowhere are hurts so hurtful or joys so joyful as they are in the ongoing contacts of enduring relationships. Each of the authors has sought for the balances between suffering and joy that are lost and found time and again in ordinary moments. Each of us has been buoyed by elation and submerged by despair over the peril and promise of relational life. And each of us has faced the risk of choosing a path where truth meets trust. Why take this risk? Why choose the way of dialogue, where trust elicits truth? After all, *I* know where *I* stand. We disagree. Why hurt each other? Why get hurt? Why bother? Why not just move on? The fundamental premise of dialogue is that each person always has a merited side. I may disagree with you. I may feel injured by you. But I cannot eclipse *your* reality. You may react to my stance. You may feel rejected by me. But you cannot invalidate *my* reality. In any case, we remain connected, unalterably linked. Direct address is the attempt to make these linkages palpable, to make relationships work.

Direct address is a tool and a stance whether or not dialogue is its end result. Nothing can guarantee dialogue between two or more relating partners, but direct address is the cornerstone of dialogic possibilities. At some point in our lives, we have been addressed. In the primal unfolding of birth and of growth, we were named and were given care. We were nurtured in our mothers' wombs, and we were provided for by the work of somebody's hands. And whatever our later interpretations of what more our parents could have done, we survived and thrived because we received. We received; therefore, we owe. We also gave; therefore, we deserve. This "will to reciprocity" (Krasner 1986, 121) is rooted in the nature of being itself, which binds us from the moment of birth with the bonds of consanguinity. This dictates obligations for both parents and children: "Just as parents become responsible for the survival of their helpless infants, children soon become accountable to the people who alone among all others gave them life" (Krasner 1986, 121). Loyalty is a hallmark of childhood (Boszormenyi-Nagy and Spark 1973). All children are driven to meet their families' expectations. Whether children are told directly or indirectly, they carry invisible loyalties, a primitive impulse that accompanies growing up. In fact, children tend to be captive to their parents' well-being. Children earn merit from their efforts to please, whether or not their parents know it. Tragedy impends when parents feel so wounded by their own parents that they are unable to see their children as giving, much less acknowledge their gifts.

The existential burden of individual and relational maturity is not a one-sided revisionist history in which we simply critique what we did or did not get, but a bold acknowledgment of what is given and what is owed. We may attack someone's parenting for its insufficiencies, but parenting by its very nature can only range from deficient to benign in each of its various dimensions. What is more critical is the question of who our parents were or are. What were the forces with which they struggled? On what resources could they count? What did they do with what they had? How did they find meaning in *their* lives? Who nurtured them? What truths informed them?

How did they ask for help, if they did? Whose hand guided them? Whose voice addressed them? Whom did they trust? To whom could they speak their truths?

The problem is this: if our parents failed to find their voice in a fair and reasoned way, what chance do we have to discover ours? In fact, in the heart of the parenting process there is a hole about which few questions are ever asked—that is, the unexamined expectations and illusions that one generation holds of another. Indelibly marked by the consequences of parental legacies and decisions, members of each generation are obliged to find healing, freedom, and a capacity to teach the process of give-and-take to children yet unborn. The success of this task rests on our movement toward direct address. Whether or not our efforts evoke a reciprocal response, we alone must decide whether or not to raise our voices and speak our truths in the trust that we will strike a responsive chord in the heart and mind of another. And at the very least we can know that our choice to speak is an attempt to balance what we owe, to assert what we deserve.

This essay will examine the concepts and applications of the ethics of direct address. It will explore the facets of a trust-based, resource-oriented stance that invites the exchange of truth in the service of just relationships, meaning making, and freedom, which come with offering due consideration to those who people our world. This work is written for anyone whose life and relationships can be repaired and restored through reentering the realm of "the between," where truth meets truth and trust becomes the mainstay of commonplace exchange. It is especially meant for those whose professional mandate requires them to provide a way for others who stand to gain meaning from the ethics of direct address.

The Longing to Connect

Ours is an era in which meaning has eroded but has not yet been eclipsed, for meaning continues to reside between those who choose to risk their truths in the crucible of direct address. It is not the role per se that elicits meaning but the intimate word that is spoken in relationships between parent and child, husband and wife, sibling and sibling, friend and friend, student and teacher, doctor and patient, worker and manager.

Direct address is the way people choose to disclose themselves to catalyze their movement toward meaning. People still want to know if there is someone to trust, if something can be done to make a difference—whatever that may be—in a time awash in a tidal wave of mammoth crises.

Ours is a time that evolved in the aftermath of Nazi Germany, Hiroshima, and Chernobyl. Environmental hazards, AIDS, street people, child suicides and murders, the threat of chemical warfare, and the mean existence that blights the underside of American and European cities and so much of Africa, Asia, and South America flood people with a penetrating and pervasive sense of helplessness, hopelessness, and meaninglessness. Ours is an age characterized by signs of new order and old violence—geographical, political, economic, individual, and interhuman. Ours is a time marked by cracks in the veneer of vision and hope. Profound disorientation and the loss of traditional and structural supports prevail and undercut the drive to sustain quality in relationships much less effect the subtle graces and demands of intergenerational family life burdened by distance, estrangement, and fragmentation.

Meaning is relational and is produced only as each person speaks his or her truth. The biological imperative is a constant reminder that people are connected. The existential challenge is how to make interhuman connections work. The transgenerational reality of sperm and egg, of male and female, of grandparent and grandchild, and of adult maturity and developmental dependency is the primal repository out of which meaning evolves. Being itself is the sine qua non of relationship, the skeletal foundation and connective tissue upon which each generation is mandated to build meaning. The self who seeks meaning is born into a transgenerational reality and into a world of relationships without which it cannot survive. All that has gone before us—biological, social, national, familial, and cultural—shapes who we are. We never exist in isolation from relationship. We never *become* in isolation from relationship. Self-containment is a myth and illusion that distances and constrains: it interrupts and circumscribes real meaning. We may choose to disengage from our families of origin, to separate from our spouses, to cut off from our children; but the reality is that we are connected. And connectedness supplies life with meaning.

Meaninglessness is produced by an unwarranted break in the connective tissue, that is, untested assumptions of insufficiency: who we are is not enough for the people around us. Personal truth that is shackled by maxims, ideologies, and other forms of untested assumptions produces unintended isolation and silent rage and despair. On the other hand, "human truth arises as one tries with his entire life to give form to his relationship to truth. And communication of human truth occurs when one takes his own side and stands up for it with his Self" (Buber 1953, 46). "The truth about something is like a string of adjectives, but the truth of something must always be experienced as a noun or pronoun" (Taylor 1971, 13); only the latter kind of communication of human truth can rightly be known as direct address. It is only this kind of truth which, unshackled and unleashed by testing one person's side against another's, can redeem despair and point a way. The capacity of the self to speak its truth in the matrix of life is the anvil upon which all meaning is fired and forged. We speak here of meaning and truth in the lived concrete, as a pulsating movement between people whose perceptions may vary but whose ground is one of a shared reality—the longing to connect.

Indirectness, circuitousness, and managed information have a cost: unintended estrangement, destructive assumptions, untested obligations, failed imagination, stunted reciprocity, psychosomatic manifestations, diminished passion for day-to-day life, unclaimed opportunities, and unrecognized contributions. Eventually, these costs can add up to a "mutual hatred system based on equal exploitation and destruction of all family members to enhance the pain that has endured from one generation to the next" (Mahan 1990). Directness also has a cost: the fear of being misunderstood, the terror of permanent disengagement, neurotic feelings of guilt attached to making a personal claim, the dread of standing alone, and risk with a questionable return. The cost of direct address is immediate and palpable. The cost of indirect address is expended over the years. But it is direct address alone that mediates "the excessive weight of the limitations which have become unbearable for us" (Buber 1953, 148).

Our common humanity has to do with the balances that exist between our passion to connect and our freedom to become. In this work, the task is to uncover and demonstrate some of the subtleties of this dual action, this biological imperative, this press to touch and to achieve, to be heard and to succeed, to trust and to create. Deep in the structure of being itself, there is a will for justice in context, a thrust toward fair consideration, and a movement toward direct address, relationship's most resourceful intervention. Deep in the structure of being itself there exists a relational ethic. Its focus is now individual, now interhuman. Its motion is always dialectical. Its domain is ever the realm of "the between." It proceeds from the premise that people are connected to one or another degree and require dialogue to hallow these connections. Dialogue incorporates two movements: (1) self-delineation—to know one's side, to embrace one's self, and to find the courage to self-disclose—and (2) due consideration—to credit and embrace the merit of another "even while I oppose him as the person that I am" (Friedman 1985, 48). Our premise here is that the justice of the human order can be rebalanced in the process of genuine address, in those brief moments of relationship when "deep calls to deep" (Buber 1965, 106). Due consideration proceeds as partner faces partner and discloses and invites. Even so, one's address to the other may remain unanswered, and the dialogue may die in seed (Friedman 1985). But the very attempt at direct address may result in self-validation, the dynamic signpost that characterizes the consequences to a person when she or he chooses to risk an investment in due consideration. By extending consideration to a partner, one not only satisfies an existing psychic need but also fulfills an ethical mandate which enhances one's own merit and worth. This act of consideration affects the balance of a person's claims and obligations. Self-validating due consideration enhances the justifiability of the self's claims on his or her world (Boszormenyi-Nagy and Krasner 1986). Whatever the outcome of direct address, the self is made more free and entitled, less burdened and neurotic. Because one has offered care, one is "allowed" to make a claim.

Deep in the structure of being itself, there is a wellspring of residual trust that supports and catalyzes authentic commitment. From generation to generation, across time, geography, class, and diverse loyalties, residual trust has provided the grace of sufficiency. It is the reservoir from which the process of exoneration and forgiveness is drawn. And it has functioned as the primary restorative element of interhuman existence. From transgenerational and intergenerational facts, residual trust draws experience, transactions, and a mutuality of commitment evidenced by long-term due consideration (Boszormenyi-Nagy and Krasner 1986). Invisible "records" of give-and-take, contributions and injuries, and the distribution of burdens and benefits within a family system develop into legacies, ledgers, and loyalties (Boszormenyi-Nagy and Spark 1973). In turn, family legacies, ledgers, and loyalties form a repository of assurance that in small measure or large confirms that a person's existence is enough. Who one is is sufficiently significant to elicit concern, attentiveness, and nurturance from those people to whom one's life has been entrusted, even in the midst of disappointment and conflict.

Residual trust then is a resource that presents itself at the outer limits of the human psyche when a person's longing to connect transports him or her to the realm of "the between" (Buber 1953). It is here between person and person that trust and truth interplay in the service of a just relationship. It is here in the arena of the interhuman that each human life is placed to address and help heal the injured order of existence. Residual trust cannot be objectified, psychologized, or theologized. It can be known only through a genuine meeting between being and being. Residual trust is the bedrock of a committed relationship. It undergirds the fragile sanctuary of the word that is spoken and the word that is heard. The terms of a committed relationship are not a hidden mystery but a truth to be embraced. When a person maintains a dialogic stance, his or her trust base deepens: the courage to address someone who may withdraw from me and the courage to receive a word that is offered when that word may assault me are acts of confirmation and expressions of esteem. I care enough about you to risk my truth in full knowledge that I may wound or be wounded. You care enough about me to receive my truth in its own context and risk joining your truth to mine. Now relational reality displaces supposition. Moving out of the domain of psychological perceptions and untested assumptions, human truth takes on "the assurance of things hoped for, the conviction of things not seen" (Heb. 11:1 RSV).

Committed relationships exist between the poles of truth and trust. The ability to make connections work is linked to a person's will to delineate his or her own truth and terms and in a parallel motion is rooted in trust, to invite and elicit the truth of another—all of this while experiencing fears and anxieties of being absorbed or abandoned. But still, in the words of Rabbi Mendel, "If I am I because I am I, and you are you because you are you, then I am I, and you are you. But if I am I because you are you, and you are you because I am I, then I am not I, and you are not you" (Buber 1961, 283). Mendel's words point to one of many characteristics of committed relating. Though the characteristics are nuanced—almost elusive—it is beneficial to attempt to list them.

1. Commitment can only be grasped through testing rather than through a monological belief or stance.

2. Commitment or the impulse toward it is motivated by a will to reciprocity (to give and take) beginning with birth itself. It is never simply a value, feeling, or principle but a relational dynamic having to do with existing in a condition of indebtedness without undue guilt.

3. Commitment is an order of giving, in trust that what is received will be valued, redemptive, reciprocated, credited, or at least duly noted, considered, and in time returned in due measure.

4. Dynamic commitment is the basis of "lived life" (Buber 1970, 89). Its methodology is a honed capacity to delineate one's own terms and to validate the merit of another person's stance, however adversarial.

5. Commitment between people is the primary dynamic measure of human meaning and the basis of interhuman ethics.

6. The glue of any just order of human existence, commitment is a sacred trust. At another time in an arguably gentler world, commitment was an assumed characteristic of personal, interpersonal, and intergenerational life. In generations past, a handshake may have sealed commitment. Today, in a world steeped in hype and a lust for "communication," a handshake may be a civil protocol or even convey a rush of feelings. The substance of commit-

ment, not the feeling or ritual behind it, is what is in question in our time.

7. The bread of just relationship, commitment is a long-term sequence of intended choices, a series of dedicated decisions to invest in a person or life circumstances with trust, freedom, and responsible response.

8. A failure of commitment is signaled by words like abuse, abandonment, exploitation, and betrayal. Commitment requires a person to move out of the psychological realm of reading or interpreting feelings and into the arena of ethical awareness to rebuild trust between one another.

9. A person's capacity to attempt to verify a relating partner's motives and justification constitutes the apex of personal freedom and interpersonal and interhuman justice.

10. Religious rituals have long been used to incarnate the meaning of commitment. Rites such as Baptism, circumcision, Communion, Bar and Bat Mitzvah, betrothal, marriage, and the Sacrament of the Sick are embodiments of commitment. As such they are ethical statements that can yield value and meaning within and between the generations if people take responsibility for seeking their truth vis-a-vis the ritual.

11. Commitment is a dialectical and dialogical way, a caring stance whose consideration for the I holds parity with consideration for the You (Krasner and Joyce 1989).

12. Relational balance is predicated on the understanding that making a claim for oneself can be an expression of giving, a contribution to the well-being of relatives and friends instead of a selfish act (Krasner 1986).

The ontology to which the characteristics of committed relating bear witness springs from the simple fact that people are connected. The bonding quality of connections notwithstanding, the tendency to withhold one's own truth and the failure to credit the truth of another are dual barriers to redemptive relating. In fact, most relating is characterized by pseudomutuality. As often as not, human interchange is superficial and is bound to form above substance, to seeming above being, and to pleasing above genuine meeting. Why do we settle for relational cut-offs, evasion, and superficiality over the inevitability of colliding truths if the human race is predisposed to a biological imperative to connect? What forces drive us away from the conviction that who we are is enough; and sufficient, we may be heard by somebody, somewhere, at some level? Why is it so hard to realize that regardless of whether or not we are heard, we are freer by virtue of having offered our word?

A person's initial feelings of insufficiency and reluctance to disclose or delineate his or her truth and to elicit that of another are consequences of the misuse of parental authority (see parentification, Boszormenyi-Nagy and Krasner 1986). The paradox is that parents who tend to expect too much of their children are typically victims in their own right. When children become captive investors in their parents' well-being, what is dynamically played out between parent and child are the unfaced, unaddressed, and often unimagined injuries that, unseen, are transposed from one generation to the next. When children are so parentified and when their parents are parentified, each generation becomes more and more obligated to the previous generation's patterns of nondisclosure, self-withholding, and personal hopelessness. As misused children, we become overresponsible adults. Overobligated, we learn not to disclose our pain, not to take personal pleasure. Depleted and weary before we begin, we learn to duck mounting assaults on our being and resources. Then we learn not to make any claims for ourselves. Finally, bitterness and silence deepen into inevitable despair. Mistrust seeps into relationships and invades and infects them. The onset of mistrust is insidious. Unaddressed, its outcome is without resolution. Self-protective boundaries are misread as defensive and selfish. When other adults fail us, we turn to our children. Then a spiral of inverted parenting begins once again.

Few people start out as wise parents. All children start out as a massive demand. But neither parent nor child is toxic by predisposition or design. Misuse of parental authority is not to be confused with organic toxicity. The fact is that there is no way for people to raise children without injuring them. The question is one of degree. The challenge of maturity comes in the adult recognition that alongside parentally imposed injury and hurt typically stand a massive investment of time, money, energy, hope, good will, actual care, and parental presence as well as a parent's deep-seated anxieties over his or her felt inadequacy and capacity to bring up a healthy child. Whatever its unavoidable fragilities and limits, parenting is from generation to generation the cornerstone of connectedness, the starting point for a new generation's ethical, spiritual, and psychological quest. The parent-child relationship is the matrix out of which all meaning flows. The volatile mix of injuries and contributions, burdens and benefits, resources and limitations, and dialogues and monologues in no way negates that "the passion of the new beginning and the ability to connect oneself to what already exists belong together. One should know most deeply: The species, generations and families which have brought me forth are carried in me; and whatever new that I do receives its characteristic meaning from that fact" (Buber 1953, 42). Real living then means that the longing to connect and the freedom to become necessitate a continuing rupture and ongoing restoration of the delicate balance between the generations, between person and person, between speaking truth and risking trust.

It is interesting that not only do people parentify their children, not only do grown children parentify their parents, but we also parentify maxims, abstractions, and heartfelt ideologies. For many of us, the relational dilemma is that we are imprisoned in a language of sacrifice and love, but we settle for the emptiness of psychological and theological abstractions. Most people embrace some form of penance and atonement. But we are typically bound up in corrosive, long-term resentment and guilt. Many people allege the saving power of an idealized parent or God's grace. But we give ourselves up to the quicksand of endless activity to justify our worth and self-esteem. Most people give lip service to a world in which everyone has a right to his or her just due. But we get bogged down in compulsive, one-sided giving in which our own just needs are rarely honored or met. Most people are invested in the wisdom of genuine forgiveness. But we quickly get stuck in a quagmire of scapegoating and blame. Most people cloak themselves in an ideology of human potential and personal growth. But we want the security of peace and healing without having to face the fear and pain that characterize a balanced, caring way. Most people exhort others to lives of vision and courage.

But we want someone to protect us from the inevitability of hurting others or being hurt. Most people support causes that espouse freedom, trust, and hope. But we are often held captive to definitions of life delimited by boundaries of pathology and sin. All of this is to say that people across the psychological and theological continuum of human existence tend to settle for too little, too fast, with too many people, especially ourselves (Boszormenyi-Nagy and Krasner 1980).

As we authors proceed to address the stuff of family life, our anchor is life, not doctrine. Our elemental stance is intergenerational and triadic: Every child is born to two parents, each of whom in turn were born to two parents and all of whom have a distinct voice and a particular truth. All of us, parent and child alike, are affected, influenced, and shaped by transgenerational relationships that have a definitive say, along with biology, on how we are men and women, on how we have been taught to connect, and on how we have gained permission to become.

Aspects of Despair

Few of us can stand in the face of a loved one's needs and not feel responsible for them, whether or not the responsibility is ours. To feel deeply and to offer help in the midst of a committed relationship may be a reasonable expression of compassion. Concern, empathy, and the longing to act on another person's behalf, whether invited to do so or not, may be a natural impulse. They are also a potential trap for acting against our own vested interests and obscuring the validity of the self's longing for pleasure—that is, the will to please another is easily pitted against our responsibility to identify what we want, to act on it, and to handle the consequences that come when our needs and wants collide.

People tend to confuse commitment with control. In fact, escalating efforts at control are essentially expressions of despair. The underlying premise is that I have lost all hope of receiving the consideration due me. As despair deepens, the option of direct address lessens, and efforts to control grow more frenzied. This frenzy usually masks a monitored rage at an unanticipated injury from a usually trustworthy source or situation. There are two injuries operating here: one is an internal reaction to the moment's disappointment; the other is the breach of trust that occurs in a relationship. But internal reactions to a moment's disappointments and breaches of trust in a relationship are ordinary phenomena that in themselves do not produce despair. They are, however, the building blocks and the natural outcome of the failure of direct address.

Despair as a condition builds up over time. It is comprised of assaults untempered by care, of one-sided giving untempered by receiving, of ascribed blame untempered by credit and confirmation. Despair is the end product of a life of obligation, which eventually erodes the hope that who we are and what we want is significant to anyone but us. It is the unyielding message that one more time our fathers are drunk, one more time our mothers are angry, one more time we cannot have friends to the house, one more time our stomachs are in knots, one more time we are expected to be silent to keep the peace at any price. In more cases than not, despair is the characteristic of dissociative loyalty that binds rather than bonds.

Let's examine aspects of despair as it was experienced in the J. family (see figure 5.1). Eileen, the firstborn daughter of Joseph and Marge, elicited her parents' basic impulse to give her everything that a newborn needs and deserves. This infant was preceded by a brother, Martin, born 12 months earlier. These children were born of parents who carried unfaced and unaddressed relational injuries, deprivations, and expectations. (Later, Joseph and Marge had three more children: Joseph, Jr., Ann, and Marie, who was born 10 years after Ann.) The dilemma that presented itself in this young family had little to do with the parents' good will to love or to trust or their desire for mutual consideration. Rather the dilemma was firmly rooted in an illusion on the part of each partner; that is, as married adults and parents, Joseph and Marge believed they had the right to something that they never managed in their families of origin—the right to control their own lives. What they perceived as helplessness and choicelessness in their families of origin was quickly transformed into unrealistic expectations and untested assumptions in their marriage and family of generation: "Finally we can do what we want to do." What happens when this man and woman suddenly discover that not only did they have little say over their lives in their families of origin, but with the birth of their first two children and the

Figure 5.1 **The J. Family**

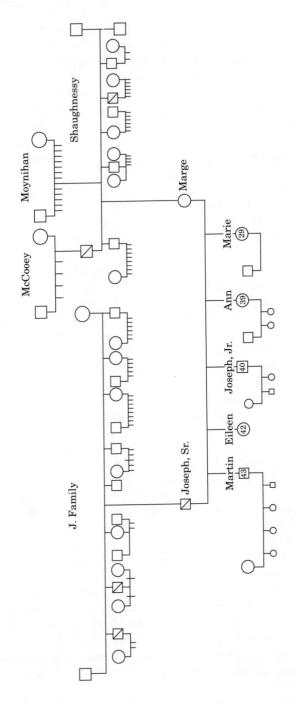

demands of infancy, work, and everyday life, they have less
and less to say over their present lives? It's almost as if they
find themselves right back in the helplessness and choicelessness they thought they had escaped.

Eileen was born with serious medical problems that required long-term hospitalizations and repeated surgeries. Her
illness induced a profound sense of helplessness on the part of
her parents, ages 26 and 25. Three years earlier, the war had
ended for Joseph, a member of a triage corps on Guadalcanal
and Iwo Jima. He returned home in search of a sanctuary from
the memories of shattered soldiers dying in his arms. He married within the year, and a year after that, Martin was born,
planned and wanted. Also welcomed, the firstborn daughter
became the fourth generation of women in her father's line to
carry the name Eileen. In constant need of attention, Eileen
was deprived of normal physiological and emotional development. She suffered from physical pain and the assaults of medical treatment. Increasingly she also suffered the loss of her
parents: Joseph distanced himself from his daughter. The
impact of his war experiences, what is now described as post-
traumatic stress disorder, left him ill prepared to endure any
further human suffering, especially that of his own infant. By
default, Marge became the accessible parent. Stretched
between Eileen's legitimate needs for nurture and care and
Joseph's increasing dismay and distress at life's circumstances,
Marge felt powerless as her hopes for control over life quickly
slipped away. Even worse, her illusion that marriage and family would put her in charge was replaced by the despairing conclusion that, once again, her life was not her own. Caught in
the legacy of a father killed at the time of her birth, an overde-
manding mother, a husband who was overresponsible first for
making his own mother's life better and then for healing soldiers who could not be healed, Marge's longing and claims for a
life of her own collapsed under the further burden of the birth
of two more children, that is, four children in 5 years.

The scene was set for the breakdown of fair give-and-take,
which characterizes all trustworthy commitment: two overresponsible parents, with four children, felt as if they had no
choices in this world. Helplessness and choicelessness, whether
real or imagined, constitute the seedbed of dependency and the
compulsion to please, to protect, and to blame. Here were six

members of a young family caught in undifferentiated pain. The hope generated for the young couple by the structures of marriage, parenthood, and family life quickly dissipated. Though structure may be an aspect of fairness in the family, it can never be a substitute for relational justice. Over time, the once-sought structure acquired the same weight as the structure from which the couple sought to escape, their families of origin. As disappointments built up in the family members, they imposed themselves upon each other. At an early age, the children were caught in their parents' conflicts. They chose sides and helped create power alliances. Unable to address each other and be heard, husband and wife turned away from each other and turned toward the child or children by whom they were most likely to be received. Drinking became Joseph's primary expression of disappointment. His sadness, anger, and silence were learned at the hands of an inaccessible father, who seemed unable even to credit Joseph for his family loyalty much less his person. Marge's disappointment expressed itself in a tendency to keep "her" children distant from "her" husband, an attempt to maximize her own possibilities of being nurtured with little thought to the long-term consequences of a father split from his children and of children who would see no demonstration of team parenting. Each felt controlled by an ever-growing sense of helplessness, made worse by unspoken expectations and accusations.

What was happening between Marge and Joseph is called a *subject-object split*: she presumed that he could hurt her but that she could not hurt him. She failed to imagine that he could carry the kind of pain that she carried. She was operating on a basis of almost nonexistent self-esteem. She did not imagine that she counted. How could he be hurt by her? Marge thought she was acting according to his expectations, and Joseph thought he was acting according to hers. Neither Joseph nor Marge credited the other because, in fact, both were carrying the resentment and blame born of having silently surrendered their own side. So when Eileen or any of the children tried to support Marge's impulse to keep peace at any price, peace never followed. In fact, Marge had no means of holding Joseph accountable for his dependent behavior, which increasingly manifested itself as alcohol addiction. She had no means of holding Eileen accountable, the very daughter who not so long ago was a symbol of promise, not of rage. How had the child of promise become a child of rage?

The vulnerability of the child was such that she could muster no sustained defense against the parents, who themselves were so defenseless. All Eileen could manage was to become visibly enraged and to attack her mother, father, and (when necessary) her siblings. But she was perceived as the powerful one in the family, an image which masked the depths of her powerlessness. After superficial examination of the J. family, an observer might condemn or even scapegoat Joseph's and Marge's parenting, but consider this later comment made by Marge, "We didn't know how to do anything else and never imagined that what we did had consequences." As Joseph and Marge grew more depleted, the young couple's mind-set was not to imagine; their mind-set was to survive. Their legacies had severely limited their capacity to identify resources in themselves and in or between each other, and the burdens of marriage and parenthood depleted whatever resources might have been there. Beyond their fantasy of the structure of marriage and family, they had nowhere to go. They did not even have the right to limit the number of children they bore. Marge was pregnant seven times in 7 years. To produce children is what Marge thought she was born to do.

Both Joseph and Marge felt isolated, injured, and vulnerable in the midst of a fierce loyalty to their children and to each other. Nevertheless, the injustices to Eileen were so profound and her longing to connect so intense that perforce she was driven into a split in order to survive: If she gave in to her longing to please, then she would further injure herself. The longer she pleased solely on somebody else's terms, the more injustice would be heaped upon her. On the other hand, if she continued to rage and to blame, she would "lose" both her parents. In other words, she was caught between silence and loss—the basic anatomy of despair. In this family, the father became the scapegoat. His drinking was identified as the cause of everyone's inner anxiety, a reflection of just how disassociated each of them had become from each other and from themselves. No one spoke from his or her own suffering ground to the suffering ground of another. Instead, each person spoke to the "problem," the manifestation of disengagement and disassociation.

Illusions of Intimacy

Genuine intimacy links our longing to connect with our freedom to unfold, and is always marked by speech-with-meaning (Buber 1965). It is steeped in a mutuality of commitment which requires trustworthy relating. Trustworthy relationships are the outcome if when we speak we mean what we say, we do what we mean, and we can rely on others to do the same. Genuine intimacy is neither a compulsion to please nor a thrust to manage information, but a will to give and take that depends on the reliability of the spoken word. Facets of intimacy are carefully nuanced by Martin Buber's description of how speech-with-meaning occurs: "whenever one showed the other something in the world in such a way that from then on he began really to perceive it; wherever one gave another a sign in such a way that he could recognize the designated situation as he had not been able to before; wherever one communicated to the other his own experience in such a way that it penetrated the other's circle of experience . . . as from within, so that from now on his perceptions were set within a world as they had not been before" (1965, 106). It is in the family that speech and meaning are first wed. It is also in the family that meaning and speech are first sundered. To be sure, even in the midst of mutual commitment, ruptures between speech and meaning and between truth and trust are inevitable. But what is retained in genuine intimacy is the conviction that whatever the reasons for the rupture, whatever its consequences, there is a clear if reluctant willingness to address them. On the other hand, a failure to address and to be addressed, to speak and to mean, and to hear and to act are signs of dissociative intimacy.

Dissociative intimacy occurs when two people are essentially connected to each other, but they cannot make the connection work. It is characterized by protectiveness of self and others, denial of pleasure, collusive silence, shame over individual creativity and achievement, and an exquisite sensitivity to the pain of others typically addressed by distancing and the refusal to take solace for oneself. It is also characterized by a subtle self-righteousness that tolerates no criticism, for example, "If I've expended so much of my existence to maintain family equilibrium, peace at any price in the midst of chaos and threat, how can I be viewed as doing anything wrong?" In the J. family, these attitudes and actions were the signposts by which Marge and Eileen indebted each other without being accountable for the consequences of their own actions. Paradoxically each member of the family felt wronged and in fact was wronged. And, at the same time, each family member remained irrevocably and inextricably connected to each other, whether they willed it or not. How then did wrongdoing take place? Joseph and Marge, like their parents before them, felt trapped in an unending spiral of obligation. Imagination failed them. They were unaware of a way to move beyond their unexamined and binding ways of relating. There was no one to credit the merit of their suffering. They felt as if everyone wanted something from them; no one was there to give, only to take. They knew nothing of their ethical right to act on their own behalf.

Given binding loyalties contracted by birth, we tend to be blindsided to the option of shaping our lives through the mechanism of choice. We tend either to settle for the fantasy of idealized relationships or to conform to the bleak prospects of relationships as they currently exist. Our stagnation is anchored in the inner construction of our psychology, that is, our own way of perceiving another person. This inner dialogue, if kept within, blocks out the possibilities of testing or inquiring into another person's reality, thereby locking out a relational partner's truth. The notion of acting on our own behalf is conceptually foreign while dynamically compelling in family and culture alike—this despite the myths of the "me generation." Birth itself endows upon every human being the need to hear and be heard, to receive and be received. The act of hearing and being heard is a necessary and, therefore, ethical right. Hearing and being heard is never a monological act. It always entails give and take. Balances between give and take are always in flux. The very act of hearing and being heard requires courage and conviction. We are schooled to please. The mechanism of direct address poses a choice between pleasing relational partners or risking self-disclosure and eliciting another person's reality. Patriotism, religion, education, work, and family collectively mystify the imperative to make discrete and considered choices. The burden of their message is always weighted by the notion that it is better to give than to receive, but the fact is that we *have* to receive in order to continue to give.

In their upbringing, Joseph and Marge were shaped by the pressure of Irish Catholic "selflessness." The negation of the self was mandatory. (1) Do not question authority: priests and nuns are always right. (2) If you do fight for what is yours, you will inevitably lose. Few, if any, youngsters could expect to complain about a teacher's unfairness and hope to be heard by their parents. (3) Your parents may fight, but rarely for themselves. (4) There may be no money for the amenities of everyday family life, but somehow 25 cents is owed to the church. (In the projects there were no pastoral calls; the priest showed up for block collection.) (5) Selfishness is accompanied by all-pervasive guilt. Asking for yourself is intrinsically indictable; giving to others is the norm and ideal. From generation to generation, Joseph and Marge learned to give themselves away—ostensibly for the kingdom of God. What they failed to learn is that asking for what seems fair is the building block of any legitimate relational vision. They had learned, as their parents before them, that they could make no direct claims on their family, their church, or their world. Their ethic was reduced to the premise that "if you make your bed, you lie in it." The very idea that people could ask for what they want, much less get it, seemed selfish and morally wrong. Their implicit relational mandate was, "Do for others, long for a return, ask nothing of anyone, take no relational risk. How is it anyway that no one knows what I want?" A son's, daughter's, husband's, wife's, father's, or mother's ethical right to speak out from an "I position" earned through due consideration was virtually nonexistent.

A child's will to please seems to begin at birth. In any case, by the end of her first year, a youngster is attuned to her parents' pain and loyal to her parents' implicit expectations. This loyalty, whether or not a parent is aware of it, constitutes a contribution on the part of the child. A child's contributions require acknowledgment. Without a parent's capacity to credit a child for loyal contributions, the youngster is subtly conformed to capitulate to one-sided expectations. Pleasing becomes a dead-end way of life, which inevitably leads to the corrosion and corruption of a fair relationship between parent and child and, by extension, between the child and her entire world. This corrosion is predicated on a child's conclusion that what she gives is never enough and that giving cannot be related to having terms of one's own. Uncredited, a child's loyal efforts toward her par-

ents deteriorates into a personal belief that "if my contributions
are insignificant, so am I." At this point, conformity, manipulation, apparent indifference, and sheer rage (with its acting-out
behaviors) become the only perceived alternatives. In this sce-
nario, dialogue is stillborn. On the other hand, the child who is
sometimes heard, sometimes credited, sometimes acknowledged
for her contributions typically develops a capacity for fair give
and take. Crediting a child at least 51% of the time stimulates
her imagination for reciprocity. In being received, she learns
how to receive. The child learns she is of consequence, significant, and has earned the entitlement to be heard, to make
choices, to disagree.

Psychologically relieved to get out of their families of origin,
Joseph and Marge were totally unprepared to indicate what
they wanted of each other or of their children—let alone to act
on their wants. Automatically conditioned to yielding their
sides, Marge and Joseph were unaware that they even had
terms. In their moves to escape the overwhelming obligation
implicit in parental expectations of them, the young couple
turned toward each other—with all their old relational patterns intact. Early on they learned that they could not survive
on their own, so they tried to take refuge in each other through
physical, psychological, and functional intimacy that overlooked their ethical rights. Theirs was a dissociative intimacy
rooted in self-denial and a monologic stance.

The connection between Marge and Eileen ostensibly began
to deteriorate around the escalating demands of Eileen's
chronic medical problems. Her illness became the visible sign
of the family's deprivation—relational, psychological, spiritual,
material, and physical. Eileen's behavior became the outward
sign of an invisible reality, that is, a signal of each family member's despair and inability to speak from his or her own suffering ground. Unable to help his daughter get well, unable to better his mother's life with his distancing, authoritarian father,
and in competition with Eileen for the attention of his wife,
Joseph saw no options for himself. Unable to imagine that he
had a right to more than what might flow from facing the
sources of his grief and loss, he pulled back into the place he
knew best. With his war experiences and the legacy of his
immigrant parents, who themselves struggled to survive,
Joseph retreated into the intimacy of alcohol, his only identifi-

able resource. Well-liked by many people, he was nevertheless bereft of a capacity to trust the adult world. Joseph clung to his 16-ounce bottle of beer as one might cling to a best friend. Marge, faced with the increasing demands of care for an ill daughter, of raising four children, and of preventing Joseph's steady retreat from the intimacy of marriage and fatherhood, trapped Eileen in a double bind: "Look at how I sacrifice for you."

Medication became an early battleground for Marge and Eileen, for the mother's offer of medicine was distant, functional, and confusing. Implied in the chaotic moments of the offer was the message, "Don't cause trouble because I can't handle it. Take the medicine and shut up." Eileen had already intuited her father's limits in terms of emotional support and connections. Now her mother's message was equally abandoning. Now Eileen was sensing her mother's limits, which rendered Eileen even more helpless in the face of Marge's constant functional availability. "Take your medicine" was not so much a token of investment between mother and daughter as it was an indirect and unheeded plea for Eileen to salve the bleeding wounds of both her parents. Paradoxically, every time Eileen took her medicine, she was muting her own voice, for the only way she found to speak was to disrupt whatever peace remained.

By the time she was nine, Eileen countered her parents in every direction, as she made her father the target of her rage. As the rest of the family did, she divided her mother and father into a "good parent-bad parent" dichotomy. She aligned herself with her older brother and found an element of nurturing there. Close in age, Martin and Eileen attended the same grade and joined forces against their father, though hers remained the designated voice. They found support in each other and were so close that they were sometimes referred to as twins. Joseph junior, 16 months younger than Eileen, stayed loyal to their father and may have been the one child whom Marge was willing to share with her husband. It was he, not his older brother, who received their father's Christian name. Could it have been Marge was replaying her unfinished legacy in the process of bestowing a name? Having lost her own father, had she claimed the first son for her own and only allowed her husband a namesake with the birth of a second son?

Eileen's raging despair was misunderstood by everyone. Still she insisted that her contributions be recognized. Though her behavior seemed delinquent, nothing escaped her vigilant thrust to establish justice in her family. In fact, one of the primary ways in which the children learned if something was amiss between the parents was to inquire as to whether Eileen was in trouble again. Her voice was a cry in the wilderness that pierced the hearts of every family member. Reduced to apparent powerlessness and even contempt in the family, Eileen was fully aware of how she split her parents and drove them further to despair. She was unaware, however, of how her younger brother hated her for destroying whatever vestige of peace there was. Eileen's unrelenting message to her mother was, "If you won't fight for me, I will fight for you. Then maybe you will learn to fight for me." She took on her mother's battles with her father and made them her own.

Eileen deliberately provoked her father. She tried to push him down the stairs. She locked him out of the house. She refused to answer the door, knowing he was there. She called the police to tell them that someone was breaking into the house, knowing it was her father. She even used her father's brother, Uncle Marty, to make her point. On one occasion, Marge had gone out to baby-sit—no small irony in itself. Bereft emotionally and relationally and overburdened with workaday responsibility, she left her own children to give her friends free time. Joseph junior recalls this incident and its impact:

> Uncle Marty had lived with us for 2 years because his siblings had thrown him out. My father was mandated by his mother to care for Marty. Marty was likable and as unentitled as my father. He had been a Seabee and lost three-quarters of his stomach to alcohol abuse. Uncle Marty lived with us for 2 years. We had a living room and a kitchen downstairs and three small bedrooms upstairs and a bathroom. Eight of us lived there, and ours was one of the smaller families in the project. Marty's presence in our home was another statement that our life together could never be on our own terms. At one point, Marty came home drunk and Eileen refused to let him in. My mother encountered a neighbor on her way home and was told that for the past 4 hours Marty had been lying in the bushes across the street, behind our row house, because he couldn't get in the house. Eileen's position was, "You're not coming in this house,

you son of a bitch," knowing that when my father came home that would start a fight. That was Eileen.

The ensuing chaos would require Marge's intervention, which signaled not so much an advocacy for Eileen but Marge's need to restore a semblance of peace as quickly as possible.

The shame and humiliation of having an alcoholic father and uncle and a mother caught between the increasing loss of marital intimacy and parental devotion left Eileen burdened with invisible loyalties. Her loyal connections to her parents and siblings and even her uncle remained intact, but they weren't working for her. Dissociated early on, Eileen was caught in an unworkable intimacy. Like her mother who fought for empty peace, Eileen was chronically caught in a raging war that silenced her cry for due consideration, fairness, and earned intimacy. For decades, Marge and Eileen were locked in a battle for control over a husband and father who was ostensibly out of control. *What no one seemed able to imagine was that, in the midst of battles for control, their commitment and their devotion to each other remained intact.* (The very fact that this commitment and devotion remain intact between people who fail to risk direct address is itself a source of ethical despair.)

Ethical Imagination: Repairing the Breach

Psychotherapy and the culture at large seem to forego the resources implicit in the ethics of direct address. Most of psychology tends to focus on pathology at the cost of crediting the loyalty ties that bond as well as bind. It seems safer to interpret a person's motives than to test one's truth against him or her. It seems easier to take a victimized stance than to initiate action on one's own behalf. It seems less trouble to psychologize than to face. Psychological perceptions, however well informed, are still internalized constructs. The limit of an internalized construct is that it in no way obligates us to imagine or to test another person's reality. It in no way asks, to say nothing of answers, the questions, "What do we owe and to whom?" "What do we deserve and from whom?" "What relationships do we need or want?" "What relationships are we obliged to retain whether or not we need or want them?" The capacity to raise these questions and to address them is the cornerstone of relational ethics. Underlying this cornerstone is the bedrock of ethical imagination.

Buber's mandate to imagine the real, to make present, to experience the other side of a relationship (inclusion) is predicated on the premise of ethical imagination. "If mutuality stirs," he says, "then the interhuman blossoms into genuine dialogue" (Buber 1965, 81). What is this ethical imagination? Buber describes it as follows:

> If we want to do today's work and prepare tomorrow's with clear sight, then we must develop . . . [a capacity for] "imagining the real," for in its essential being this gift is not a looking at the other, but a bold swinging—demanding the most intensive stirring of one's being—into the life of the other. This is the nature of all genuine imagining, only that here the realm of my action is not the all-possible, but the particular real person who confronts me, whom I can attempt to make present to myself just in this way, and not otherwise, in his wholeness, unity, and uniqueness, and with his dynamic centre which realizes all these things ever anew.
>
> Let it be said again that all this can only take place in a living partnership, that is, when I stand in a common situation with the other and expose myself vitally to his share in the situation as really his share.

In the J. family, displays of commitment and devotion lacked the infusion of direct address. Family members were bereft of the tool of ethical imagination that alone could begin to repair the breaches that stood between them. Try as she may, Eileen could not impact her father's drinking. Joseph's drinking could not impact Marge's efforts to secure peace at any price. Marge's one-sided giving was never enough to stanch her husband's and children's resentment. The more self-sacrificing she was, the more parentified she became. Marge could never do enough; the more overburdened she was, the more infantilized were the other family members who did not act for themselves. The children tried to protect their mother by staying silent: "I'm not going to ask for anything. I'll be good so you don't have to worry about me."

Over time Eileen and Martin interpreted their father's emotional inaccessibility as rejection. They decided that he was their father through biology alone. Though Joseph was reliable with his infant children, he reverted to behavior absorbed in his family of origin as they grew. The fourth child of nine, Joseph felt unattended, unchosen, and unembraced. At the time of Joseph's birth, his father was 41. Joseph's father had immigrated from Ireland at 18 years of age and married at age 35. Had his father become depleted in those years? Why did Joseph delay his own marriage? Who was in Joseph's care during that time? Did the father's inaccessibility imprint on Joseph the mark of his own insignificance? Was Joseph's withdrawal from his own children a further expression of how unnecessary he felt?

Joseph junior decided that his mother had no more power to protect him than he had to protect his mother. He internalized his parents' suffering by bringing a raging intensity to everything he encountered. Only 100% was possible. No compromise was imaginable. Joseph junior concluded that if he wanted something done he would have to do it himself. No one could be relied on. What's more, if something had to be done, it had to be done for others. Joseph junior lost the capacity, if ever he had it, to even consider doing something for himself. He could accomplish objectives, but he could not become an object for his own investment. He could earn college degrees and accolades in sports. He could buy a house and prove his independence and self-sufficiency. But he could claim no personal ground in which to plant the seeds of his own success. Moreover he converted all of life into obligation. Duty precluded pleasure, and Joseph junior was never free to take for himself.

Ann eventually replicated her parents' marriage by leaving the house, finding a man whose neediness was akin to her father's neediness for her mother, and thus established a channel for her own need to be needed. Loyal to her mother's unfulfilled wish for marital consideration, Ann overgave to her husband with the unsurfaced hope that he would eventually take care of her on her terms. It never happened. Marie had permission to love her father openly. Freer than her siblings to express her devotion to him, she nonetheless struggled with an inability to surface her side. She was graced by a 10-year gap between her birth and Ann's. Marie received parenting from Joseph senior, from Marge, who was working, and from her siblings as well. The irony of Marie's life is that, despite the

inpouring of her family's caring investments, she was inclined
to interpret the world through a negative stance. Was she
defending herself against her siblings' and parents' splits and
deprivations?

As young adults, the J. children stood on the verge of their
own adult lives. They took their unaddressed rage and resources
on the next step of the journey. What they began to applaud as
independent decision making on their own behalf was really an
expression of the isolation and loss of intimacy that each had
experienced in their family and culture. Their collective effort,
like their parents' before them, was to say, "This is my life. No
one will tell me what to do." But neither continued self-isolation
nor ongoing attempts to control others as a means of self-defense
provided a viable matrix for ethical imagination. In the absence
of direct address and ethical imagination, members of the J. family were unable to rely on the fact that commitment, devotion,
and residual trust lay latent in their connectedness—waiting to
be tapped and used for personal gain and growth as well as for
the consideration of others.

Few of us seem able to balance our passion for connection
with our freedom to unfold. But without the courage to disclose
our own terms and the ethical imagination to envision
another's, relationships cannot be made to work. The reality of
our lives is that we are connected to what already exists.
Inarguably, "the species, generations and families which have
brought me forth, are carried in me and whatever new that I
do, receives its characteristic meaning first from that fact"
(Buber [1948] 1963, 45).

In large measure, Joseph's and Marge's context is every person's context. Their lives reflect the commonalities that characterize family life:

The passion to connect is always present.

The dilemma at hand is what to do with interhuman connections as they currently stand. How does a person act
on his or her own behalf and criteria as well as address
other people and their life priorities?

Split loyalties, that is, being caught between seemingly conflicting expectations, prevent family members from
redeeming their connections.

Split loyalties are directly connected to unfaced, unreworked family loyalties from generation to generation.

Neither parent has the imagination to identify the residual indebtedness and rage that continues to bind them to their own parents.

Both parents believe they are accountable to their parents but cannot imagine that their parents are also accountable to them.

Marge and Joseph try to use the criterion by which they were raised (loyalty expectations) as a point of reference for their own children. This fails. The children have their own context and criteria.

Marge and Joseph's young-adult children want "something more" and look to a shifting society to redress their grievances.

Relational injustices in the family are linked to societal and cultural upheaval in the sixties. John Kennedy is killed. The war in Vietnam escalates.

Legitimate authority falls out of fashion. Rights become a rallying cry. Indebtedness, which constitutes one pole of the balance between rights and responsibility, is held in contempt. Fair give-and-take is bypassed or ignored. Police officers are defined as pigs; government is characterized as subversive; all manifestations of institutional life are seen as corrupt; and the family as an entity is viewed as irrelevant.

External criteria like roles and structure, custom and ritual, have been questioned, impacted, and reshaped by personal longings, which are poured into social movements opposing the status quo.

Sources of meaning, grounded in history and legacy, in trust and reciprocity, are beclouded.

The "me generation" begins to unfold, more likely motivated by despair than by selfishness: If we can't count on people to hear us or credit our side, if differences are so much more significant than commonality and trust, then better to withdraw and try to construct an artificial world—one which promises greater control and accessible nurturing.

What can be said about these commonalities of family life? Meaning and the very reason for being are produced by what has gone before us. When members of a generation shut themselves off from facing and addressing the influence of all that happened before their time and which in fact brought them forth, they find themselves without moorings in the living stream of tradition. Their drive to give form to things no longer has any connectedness to the primary reality of being itself (Buber 1953). Without connectedness to the primary reality of being itself, which might be catalyzed by direct address from one family member to another, by one genuine friend to another, by a corporate mentor to the young in his or her charge, we have a world adrift—whatever its veneer. We have a world where personal passion is prostituted. We have a society in which despair at being heard deteriorates into a compulsive search for methods to narcotize the soul.

Ethical despair is a flight from direct address. Ethical imagination is a decision to build trust through disclosing one's truth and inviting another's. How did members of the J. family eventually turn from a condition of despair to a situation of ethical imagination, from individual chaos to interhuman consideration? Developmentally, high school graduation was a launching pad for permission to enter the military, go to college, get a job. Martin went into the military. Eileen got a job and moved out of her parents' home. Joseph junior stayed at home and went to college. Ann worked, moved in with Eileen, and eventually married. Marie was still in grade school. Early on, the siblings learned that to get what they wanted they had to rely on themselves. Over time the family members began to assess the impact of their family of origin on their present day-to-day life. In their expanding contracts with an extended community at work, at home, and at play, they began to react to some of the same imbalances of give-and-take that they had suffered earlier in their lives. Anxieties and fears began to reemerge. Resentments and old feelings of guilt started to repeat and replay. What did they have to do to be heard and cared for on terms of their own? Would they always be in debt to somebody else's needs and demands?

When Joseph junior was 25, he became depressed and suicidal. Achievement was nice but had lost its thrill. Accomplishments no longer produced enough meaning to make him want to live. He began to travel to look for meaning. He searched religion to discover a healing word. In Switzerland he listened to one more tiresome lecture, but this time a chord was struck. He was suddenly hit by the revelation that relationship was more than obligation. Joseph junior began to intuit the resources in his family, whereas before he had only identified pain. A transforming event had occurred. Energized by the moment, he was impelled to return to his family members to begin the awkward and clumsy motions toward direct address. In the process, Joseph junior began to tap into the benefits as well as the burdens of his family's lives. During the transition into adulthood, the J. siblings had created an interdependent network among themselves and with their peers. Moreover, an unrecognized resource at the time was their parents' mutual devotion to each other as well as to their children, which remained intact despite marital separation. Their commitment and devotion may have warped, buckled, and bent, but never ceased. In the midst of a society in which everything seemed up for grabs, these family members were imprinted with a message of connectedness. The siblings knew the legitimacy of their parents' hopes as well as the sometimes squalid facts of their parents' lives. But where was the mentor to guide them into another mode of existence? How would they begin to imagine how to do for themselves what their parents were unable to make work? How could they avoid holding their parents in contempt and blaming them for injuries imposed? How would the siblings come to imagine their parents' palpable contributions side by side with their more obvious limits and failings?

Tapping Residual Trust

How is it that a person becomes motivated to seek healing and direct address? Buber describes the motivation in terms of *limit* and *unlimitedness*: "We break out and reach with both hands into the dark, grasping for an . . . unlimited truth. We petition, we entreat for it. . . . Unlimitedness does penetrate our limit, presses through into it. . . . This breaking out of the human person in the encounter with truth is that which brings resolution and makes the path turn. It is the birth of the soul in the human and in humankind, ever anew. Our time and its young people have estranged themselves from this fact" ([1948]

1963, 45). The excessive weight of unbearable limitations in a person's life is always a motivational factor in his or her choice to enter therapy. In the J. family, for example, it was Joseph junior, the third born, whose rage and desperation had become an unbearable weight. Six months after his father's death, Joseph junior called his family together to help him walk through his grief. Four years later, family members continue to address each other, sometimes sporadically and sometimes consistently, sometimes in dyads and sometimes all together—but in any case an irreversible process has begun.

"When my father died," Joseph junior said when he first began therapy, "a part of me died." What part of you died?" he was asked. "The pull to make life okay for my father," he responded. "The pressure to skip my life in order to help him live his." Joseph's grief at his father's death was tempered by relief, but his relief at diminished responsibility was mixed with terror at finally facing the option of leading a life of his own. It seemed clear to people around him that Joseph had a life of his own: he was married, had children, and was engaged in a successful career, but, in fact, his inner mandate was to "caretake" others and, in the process, to abandon himself. A year later he was to tell his mother that he had been suicidal. She was stunned to learn that he had limits, to say nothing of despair. She could barely grasp the fact that Joseph's efforts to stay loyal to his parents had almost cost him his life.

Joseph, Jr.: As I went along, it was hard for me to own my own degrees or accomplishments. I was still trying to get your and Dad's acceptance of what I was doing.

You didn't know what I was looking for, and I didn't know what it was at the time. Worse, the more I accomplished, the more distance came between us. Not just you and me but the whole family.

Therapist: Were you ashamed of your accomplishments, Joseph?

Joseph, Jr.: I was certainly embarrassed by them.

Marge: But they were earned the hard way. Aren't you proud of that?

Joseph, Jr.: I was. But it wasn't enough.

Therapist: I wonder who in the family told Joseph how uncomfortable you were with him. I wonder if anyone said, "Hey wait a minute. What in the hell are you doing that for? I feel disconnected from you. Help me understand your truth." Then Joseph might have said, "I don't understand your truth either." You might have been confused by each other or disagreed with each other. But you might have reconnected and not been so alone.

That's what Joseph means, Marge, when he talks about his education obscuring his truth. His accomplishments essentially cut him off from the people he loved, who then began to call him "rigid" and "formal."

Periods of unbearable weight are part of all of our lives; how we address these periods determines whether cut-offs or trust will characterize us in future modes of relating.

Parent and offspring can misunderstand, wound, and undercut each other. They can tear down all visible evidence of trust between them, but their linkages remain. It is these linkages that function as the reservoir of residual trust. Liking, approving of, or agreeing with each other is not the primary basis of their invisible attachment. Rather it is caring—given, received, and documented in the predetermined facts of conception, pregnancy, and survival—that provides the cornerstone for their mutuality of commitment, the mortar for building a sturdier foundation, and the basic potential for meaning between person and person. Fully turned and radically open to each other, the parent and the child who truly meet are strengthened by their course (justice) and lent courage by their source (residual trust).

Residual trust can never be confined, delimited, or reduced. It lies latent in the substream of enduring relationships, waiting to be tapped. It needs to be identified, however. Residual trust is most readily identified in the midst of the lingering devotion and of the amorphous commitments of family members, who are irrevocably linked by ties of root and legacy. It is never to be found in some pure or idealized way of feeling. To the contrary, residual trust is typically to be mined in the depths of volatile passions and in the midst of forbidding injustices, pathology, and mistrust (Krasner 1986).

Between the options of commitment and the impositions of control, where does residual trust fit in? At a conscious level,

we people opt for a controlling stance out of a transgenerational mandate that says we have a role, function, and place in
life which preclude the personal ground through which to connect and unfold. Inevitably, however, role, function, and place
become static and, when they remain unexamined and unaddressed, become sources of rage, resentment, guilt, and ethical
disengagement (Boszormenyi-Nagy and Krasner 1986). In-
exorably, and in our own time, we crash into the stone wall of
unbearable weight and excessive limitations that is produced
by life's ordinary demands: marriage, parenthood, filial concern
for aging parents, profession and job, social expectations, and
economic realities, to say nothing of life crises such as sickness,
death, separation, and loss. It is at points of chronic overload
that the inner gnawing of meaninglessness threatens to deteriorate into despair. It is at the moment when we intuit that we
can give no more without getting in return, or when we perceive ourselves as giving without sufficient return, that the
very fabric of day-to-day existence unravels, and meaning dis-
appears.

It sometimes seems that only when life's apparent foundations crack and are laid bare that we can finally let go of the
illusion of control and choose the invisible resources of trust,
which reside in all long-term commitment. In fact, all authentic commitment is resourced by residual trust, enabled by ethical imagination, and catalyzed by ongoing attempts at direct
address—mounted in the face of anticipated rejection, dis-
missal, and rebuff. From generation to generation, residual
trust has provided the grace of sufficiency, that reservoir from
which the process of forgiveness can begin. From generation to
generation, residual trust has been the primary restorative element of interhuman existence. A person's ability to identify,
mobilize, and catalyze residual trust offers a counterweight to
individual and relational limits, stagnation, and disengagement produced by festering blame of self as well as others and
massive rage linked to unexamined and untested family patterns, myths, and assumptions.

Restoring a Dialogic Way

In the J. family, Joseph junior's claim on his mother to hear
and be heard is founded on the bedrock of residual trust intrin-

sic to their connectedness, and has redemptive ramifications not only for them but for their relationships with everyone in their past, present, and future.

Marge: As a result of my coming here, not the easiest thing in the world to do, I've thought of a lot of things that were probably way, way back in the back of my mind and never brought forward.

I can really and truly look at my own mother probably for the first time, and not just see her as a stone, as a rigid person. I can't believe after all these years that I am looking at her in a different light now. And it's all because of my talking with Joseph, what we have talked about within the family. I know and see and probably understand her for the first time. I mouthed the words before, but now . . . I feel better. I don't think I was better. I feel now like I did when my daughter discovered my breast cancer. I was finally caught, and I was going to have to go to the doctor.

Now I'm caught again, and I have to look at things. My mother's position in our family always bothered me, evidently much more than I knew.

Therapist: How would you identify your bitterness at your mother, Ms. J., and what has come clearer for you?

Marge: I discovered that I was the only one in the family who never had a job during high school; I never did anything. Did my mother think I was a total incompetent?

My sister baby-sat at age 13. She was 5 years younger than I. My mother was a widow; then she remarried. These are my half brothers and sisters, but I have always been very, very close to them. It was during the depression. My family had lost their home. They had lost everything. Certainly we could have used the money, but I wasn't allowed to baby-sit.

Therapist: Do you know why?

Marge: I have no idea. It was just something with my mother. She went from being a princess to being this woman in a house with seven children. She struggled to keep up appearances. Appearances were always important to my mother.

Therapist: Was your mother's attitude toward you different from what it was toward the other children?

Marge: By the time the others were growing up, the family was financially well on their way. I can't find an explanation for it unless it was because, back in those days, a woman who had children and then remarried may have been looked on with contempt. I know Daddy's family did not like my mother. I didn't find that out for many, many years.

Therapist: Your stepfather's family?

Marge: Yes. He's the only father I ever knew. We used his name, but my brother and I were never legally adopted by him. My mother did not want that. I often thought about why we used his name. Before my mother died, I got up the nerve to ask her. I said, "Mom, why didn't you ever have us legally adopted?" From a legal point of view, it presented a problem. When I went to work for the government, it presented a problem. It presented a problem for my brother when he went into the service. She said that she felt the kids would be closer if they didn't know that their fathers were two separate men.

Joseph, Jr.: In view of Grandmother's losses, she was probably overprotective of Ed [Marge's brother] and you. I can imagine the emotional dependency that must have formed between you and Grandma.

Therapist: Was your mother possessive of you, Ms. J.? Did she cling to you? Was she afraid to let you out of her sight?

Marge: I obviously fed into it. I didn't even handle my own paycheck when I went to work. I would cash the paycheck, get candy for my little brothers and sister, and come home and give it to my mother. I thought nothing of it then. I could get things for myself if I wanted them. But I can remember Daddy repeatedly saying, "Coletta, you have got to let Marge handle her own money."

Therapist: Are you saying your mother babied you?

Marge: Yes. I think she did. That actually made me a less-than-responsible person.

Therapist: Maybe you let yourself be babied to protect your mother. Knowing she clung to you, it may have been too hard to grow up. And too hard for her to have you grow up.

Marge: In her mind we must have been two separate families. Edward and I were one family. The other five children were another family.

Joseph, Jr.: It sounds like Grandma was caught in a split loyalty, the way you were caught between Dad and us growing up.

Marge: (nods her head yes)

Joseph, Jr.: I wonder if part of Grandma's motivation for not letting you be legally adopted was to preserve the integrity of the name of the family bloodline. Was it Moynihan?

Marge: My real name? It was McCooey.

Joseph, Jr.: Grandma was never invested in her first husband's family. Still she had you keep their name.

Marge: Well your birth certificate, my birth certificate, all record my name as Margaret Eileen McCooey.

Joseph, Jr.: Oh, okay.

Marge: And Coletta Moynihan and Francis McCooey are listed as my parents even though, in reality, I never knew my own father.

I was 21 when I had to sign a paper to release $500 to me from the accident in which my real father was killed. The money was assigned to Margaret Eileen McCooey, but the lawyer had me sign Shaughnessy, with McCooey in parentheses. My mother would not discuss it. She just pressed me to spend the money then and there. We went down to the May Company in Cleveland and bought a bedroom set I could not stand. But it was what she wanted. So I said, "Knock your socks off; it doesn't make any difference to me."

Therapist: I'm wondering to what degree you and your older brother represented your mother's only connection to your father. To what degree did she keep you separate because she didn't want to finally lose him?

Marge: I never really got any feeling from her about her marriage.

Therapist: Was your mother an expressive person?

Marge: Not really.

Therapist: Did she speak warmly of her second husband?

Marge: There was a little more there. Her second husband was a professional person.

Therapist: Maybe her second marriage was a better financial arrangement. It must have been terribly hard for a young woman to have two babies and lose her husband.

Marge: When Joseph graduated from high school and we got his photograph, I remember saying, "Wait until your Grandma sees this picture." Joseph is the spitting image I have of my real father.

Therapist: Joseph, do you know that picture?

Joseph, Jr.: No.

Marge: Remember, there's a very old newspaper from 1922?

Joseph, Jr.: I just don't recall.

Marge: I'm going to get it out because I want you to see it. I think it's important.

Therapist: I want to jump a minute and ask how you relate to your daughter, Eileen, Marge. Do you see parallels between how you relate to your daughter and how you related to your mother?

Marge: First of all, you have to know Eileen. She's a very unique person. She's very willful, too. She was never anyone you could get real close to. She would give you the shirt off her back, but there was always a price tag on it.

Joseph, Jr.: I think there are parallels between your relationship with Eileen and your relationship with Grandma, for example, your dependency on your mother and Eileen's dependency on you. In both cases, there are very loyal daughters who never learned to ask for anything for themselves.

Marge: But Eileen is a very intimidating person.

Therapist: And you back away from her?

Marge: I back away from a lot of things. I just don't like arguments. I know it's the coward's way out. Confrontations are great if you're talking to people who can look at things logically. But when you don't have control of your own life, how can you confront someone else?

Joseph, Jr.: Eileen can be intimidating. But she's also shut down. I guess in my own pain I assumed that my whole family was suffering, too. But I haven't always credited them for their suffering. When we came into therapy, it was really the first time I could imagine how much it cost Martin to be the firstborn. Now I know he shut down to survive, and maybe he's shut down for life. I remember his migraines and things like that. But the first therapy session was one of the first times that I could imagine what it cost him. Even so, it pisses me that he still doesn't call.

In a small and halting manner, family members begin to address each other, finally aware that silence has had too high a cost.

Direct address is built on the foundation of residual trust. A mother's willingness to be addressed by her son, a brother's willingness to consider his siblings' pain and still hold on to his own legitimate expectations, all converge over time to tap into the resource side of human existence and interdependency. At intimate levels of relating, timidity of each human spirit is to be presumed. Nevertheless, the very act of facing comprises both a prologue and an epilogue that witness to the presence of residual trust, resting in the ground of existence, waiting to be tapped and claimed.

In Marge's decision to face Joseph junior, she not only began the process of healing past wounds and opening up new options for the future, but she also found new degrees of freedom to reengage her own parents in dialogue, though they were long since dead. Her son's claim on her and her willingness to address him also helped her face Eileen. In facing Eileen, she began to differentiate between her ledger with her mother and her ledger with her eldest daughter (Boszormenyi-Nagy and Spark 1973); between her ledger with her biological father, her ledger with her stepfather, and her ledger with her dead husband, whom she alternately described as the problem and as the only person in her life to whom she could ever really talk. In tapping the residual trust that lay invisibly between them, every member of the J. family, whatever the degree of their engagement with each other, was reminded that direct address is a living, if frightening, process in which "something previously unthinkable has become thinkable and expressible, and this something belongs to the category of the unforeseeable things which renew the world" (Buber [1948] 1963, 45).

References

Boszormenyi-Nagy, I., and B. R. Krasner. 1980. Trust-based therapy: A contextual approach. *American Journal of Psychiatry* 137: 767–75.

————. 1986. *Between give and take: A clinical guide to contextual therapy.* New York: Brunner/Mazel.

Boszormenyi-Nagy, I., and G. M. Spark. 1973. *Invisible loyalties: Reciprocity in intergenerational family therapy.* Hagerstown, Md.: Harper and Row.

Buber, M. [1948] 1963. The prejudices of youth. Trans. O. Marx. In *Israel and the world: Essays in a time of crisis*, 41–52. New York: Schocken.

————. 1953. Die vohiele der jugend. In *Hinweise: Gesammelte essays.* Zurich: Manesse Verlag. Unpub. trans. by P. Schaefer.

————. 1961. *Tales of the Hasidim: The later masters.* New York: Schocken. Original German edition published 1948.

————. 1965. *The knowledge of man: A philosophy of the interhuman.* Trans. M. Friedman and R. G. Smith. New York: Harper and Row. Original German edition published 1923.

————. 1970. *I and thou.* New York: Scribner.

Friedman, M. 1985. *The healing dialogue in psychotherapy.* New York: Aronson.

Krasner, B. R. 1986. Trustworthiness: The primal family resource. In *Family resources*, ed. M. A. Karpel, 116–47. New York: Guilford Press.

Krasner, B. R., and A. J. Joyce. 1989. Male invisibility: Breaking the silence. *Journal of Christian Healing* 15:14–17.

Mahan, J. 1990. Letter to my daughters. Unpublished letter, Philadelphia, Penn.

Taylor, J. V. 1971. *The go-between God.* London: SCM.

6

Metaphors, Models, Paradigms, and Stories in Family Therapy

Alvin C. Dueck

Ethics is the ubiquitous topic of conversation among mental health professionals these days. Consumer complaints, malpractice suits, professional image, and blatant violations have served to heighten the expectation that professional promise and practice coincide. It is no surprise, then, that ethics committees of professional organizations at both the state and national level report an increase in consumer complaints.

Sometimes our conversation about ethics is little more than professional turf building. At other times it is an abstract discussion about which ethical principles might be applied in situations involving ethical quandaries. Occasionally ethics is synonymous with custom, little else. Then there are times when the ethical exchange is concerned about the welfare of the client and the larger community. In the last analysis, ethics in therapy must be more than protectionism, abstract principles, etiquette, and a grab bag of techniques to avoid lawsuits. While the literature concerned with ethics and individ-

175

ual therapy has burgeoned (Keith-Spiegel and Koocher 1985; Kottler and Van Hoose 1977), reflection on ethics and family therapy is just beginning to emerge. Apart from scattered (Green and Hansen 1989; Piercy and Sprenkle 1983; Simon 1989; Wendorf and Wendorf 1985; Woody 1990) but significant articles (Margolin 1982), there are only two texts on family therapy and ethics, one an edited collection (Hansen and L'Abate 1982) and the other a book-length treatment of ethical issues in family therapy (Huber and Baruth 1987).

The ethical problems that preoccupy family therapists include confidentiality, paradoxical intervention, therapist neutrality, minority values, competency, family health, role expectations, and so on. Should spouses be made aware of information shared in individual sessions? Is the manipulation of client behavior ethical? Do therapists unavoidably impose their values on families? What is the family ideal assumed by the therapist? What are the role expectations of male and female clients held by the family therapist? As important as these issues are for family therapists, they are not the focus of this essay. Rather, my concern is with the *pretheoretical* commitments that seem to determine therapists' ethical responses in the process of therapy.

Among family therapists, there appears to be no consensus as to the role of ethics in the process of therapy. For example, there is an ongoing debate among therapists regarding neutrality and the imposition of values. On the one hand, some family therapists maintain the fundamental neutrality of their therapy. Cloé Madanes (1981) and Jay Haley (1976) both claim that their interventions are value neutral. Her therapy, Madanes asserts, is based on common sense. Neutrality in this context means that the therapist functions in a relationship equidistant to each member of the family. Moralism and judgment are avoided. Neutrality guarantees that no one perspective (the therapist's or a family member's) predominates. On the assumption that the family has the resources to create change, to set its own course, the Milan group uses language that encourages therapists to respect the autonomy of the family. Laurie MacKinnon and Dusty Miller restate this position: "The therapist maintains a meta-position to family members, their beliefs, their patterns of interaction, and avoids taking a position for or against behavioral change. This position excludes any prejudice concerning class, race, ethnicity, social norms and any concerns about illness or pathological diagnosis. The therapist avoids entering into anything more than fleeting coalitions with family members and, by the session's end, should be experienced by the family as equally aligned with each member" (1987, 147).

Some family therapists, on the other hand, are clearly directive and consider value neutrality to be a myth. Salvador Minuchin (1974, 1984) and Murray Bowen (1978) fall into this category. Both maintain a tight control on what transpires during the therapeutic hour, and their interventions are clearly driven by ideological stances. Arguing that ethical considerations in family research and therapy are unavoidable (see Browning 1988a), advocates of this position maintain that ethics is involved in the image constructed of the normal family, for example, its structure, roles, function, story, and distribution of power. They would assert that the one held responsible for family pathology reflects an ethical position, not simply a description. Is the pathology a reflection of societal norms, or is the mother to blame? What roles are appropriately expected of family members? What parental behaviors are considered appropriate and inappropriate? All of these questions require responses that are ethical in nature. (Though, as a therapist, I accept the inevitability of ethical issues in therapy, this does not mean that values are automatically imposed.)

Metaphors, Models, and Paradigms

In this essay, I will examine the moral texture of family therapy and then turn to religious ethics. Through the moral dimension, the implicit ethical expectations of the family within Western culture are examined. The biblical story of the reign of God serves as a point of departure for the section on religious ethics and the family. The tenor of the section on morality is more universal, while the section on religious ethics is more particular. My thesis is that ethics in family therapy is evidenced in a number of different ways:

1. by the implicit *metaphors* used to describe the family and construct interventions,
2. by the implicit *models* of the family, embedded in the larger social context, that shape therapeutic interventions,

3. by the implicit ethical *paradigms* that are the basis of some therapeutic approaches, and
4. by the particular religious *story* and social practices that reflect the family therapist's primary community.

In the first section of this chapter, I view ethics from the perspective of the moral metaphors, models, and paradigms that govern family theory and therapy (Barbour 1974). I would like to suggest that the metaphors family therapists bring to their work shape the nature of their interventions. Some therapists assume that the family is like an "idea," in that the family constructs its own identity much as a writer constructs a paragraph—both are acts of creation. Other therapists liken the family to a well-oiled machine, a troupe of actors, or an unfolding organism. The decision to focus ideological construction on one rather than another metaphor is a decision that has ethical implications. After all, a metaphor shapes prescription. In a pluralistic society, however, to assume that therapy is prescriptive is problematic; hence, distinctions between family therapists are reframed in this chapter as theoretical issues rather than ethical commitments.

Not only do metaphors shape the process of family therapy, models of the family implicit in a culture also serve as ethical markers for the process. For example, role definitions within the family based on gender are reinforced by society. How the conflict of individual rights and family obligations is negotiated is in part scripted by the social milieu. Thus, when one considers the individualistic nature of our culture (Bellah et al. 1985), it would follow that ethical prescription favors differentiation from families of origin over reintegration. Ethical paradigms are larger systems that guide the therapeutic process. I will examine the enlightenment paradigm of Ivan Boszormenyi-Nagy (Boszormenyi-Nagy and Krasner 1986; Boszormenyi-Nagy and Spark 1973; Boszormenyi-Nagy and Ulrich 1981). Few family therapists discuss the ethical principles or convictions that shape their approach to therapy as systematically as Boszormenyi-Nagy and his colleagues have done. For them, moral principles of justice and contract shape both theory and therapy.

Implicit Ethical Metaphors in Family Theory and Therapy

Family therapy is an ethical process because it provides and reinforces metaphors with which a family and therapist can live. Regardless of the metaphor used by the family or the therapist, each metaphor has an implicit ethical mandate. The difference between theories as we find them in the family therapy literature is not simply a matter of cognitive orientation but also a consequence of an implicit ethical position. Each family therapist reflects the possibilities of action within the parameters of a particular metaphor. To this extent, family therapy is ethical.

The metaphors that shape the theories and practices of family therapy are implicitly ethical, and the presence of implicit ethical metaphors in the theories is not inherently unethical. However, not admitting that one's biases are ethical is problematic. Moreover, to be ethical is not to argue that any one metaphor is more ethical than another. Rather, in therapy different ethical metaphors are acceptable, depending on the situation and the primary narrative of the family therapist. In the 1944 book *World Hypotheses*, which contains an analysis of four major metaphors that shape Western metaphysical and ethical thought, Steven Pepper suggests that the complex array of metaphysical thought can be reduced to formism, mechanism, contextualism, and organicism. Each metaphor is rooted in experience and suggests certain ethical injunctions. In fact, some of the differences in the various theories of family therapy can be understood in terms of these metaphors. In the precess of reviewing the metaphors and family therapy theories, I hope to uncover the implicit ethical assumptions as well. Table 6.1 outlines the various metaphors, the family theory most influenced by each metaphor, and each metaphor's implicit ethical injunction.

Formism. The core metaphors of formism include the commonsense intuition of similarity and difference, the artisan who makes something according to a plan, or the growth of natural objects according to some plan (Pepper 1944). The formistic metaphor construes the person in terms of rationality and ideation. Reason is what distinguishes us from the animals. Ideas are innate, not based on experience; thus, reason

Table 6.1 Core Metaphors, Family Therapy Theories, and Ethical Injunctions

Metaphor	Core Metaphor	Family Therapy Theory	Ethical Injunction
Formism	Idea	Constructivist	Think differently
Mechanism	Machine	Strategic	Act differently
Contextualism	Actor	Existential	Individuate
Organicism	Relationship	Structural	Connect differently

is given primacy over experience. In the words of René Descartes, "Cogito ergo sum" (I think, therefore I am).

Formism is represented by constructivists like George Kelly (1969). This not-so-new position argues that the social reality of a family is a cognitive construction. The family does not see what is really out there, but through language the family is able to construct a social world that gives meaning to the family's style of existence (Bagarozzi and Anderson 1988; Reiss 1981). This rationalist way of construing reality is in the tradition of Pepper's formists.

The formistic metaphor shapes our understanding of the family through the descriptions of various normative stages through which all families pass (Augsburger 1989) and which become the criteria against which all families can be judged. The stages are rationally constructed, and the family is then evaluated for adequacy on the basis of similarity to a given stage. The metaphor also manifests itself in the importance given to rationality in controlling anxiety in the family system. Bowen (1978) makes a radical distinction between reason and emotion and suggests that reason is the distinguishing mark of what it means to be human. His response to the lack of emotional differentiation in families is a nonanxious presence (read "calm rationality").

Prescription follows the ethical implications of the primary metaphor. For the constructivists, change in families is a function of altering how members think rather than altering the way families relate or their socioeconomic contexts. The temptation for those who use this metaphor exclusively is to view distress as a function of a family's construction of reality rather than of more objective factors, such as racism, sexism, poverty, or unemployment. The choice to focus on rationality rather than on economics or other social factors emanates from the primary metaphor.

The primary metaphor does more than simply organize our thoughts about the family and its members. Because of the depth with which the metaphor functions in the human psyche, it also shapes behavior and tends to create an aura of normativity. Pepper comments on the ethical implications of the formistic metaphor:

> Human and social norms are ethical standards of value. In concrete existence, especially among the more complex forms of existence, these norms seem to exhibit states of human and social equilibrium, and serious distortions are accompanied by discomfort and pain. Hence Plato's search for the perfect State, Aristotle for the several types of social structure exhibiting a golden mean, and the search of many modern men [humanity] for the life cycle of a normal culture, or for the normal stages of transition of culture toward the perfect social structure. All such studies presuppose formistic categories. For no other world hypothesis supports the reality of norms as laws determining (even though not always without interference) the concrete course of existence. (1944, 179–80)

That the formistic metaphor has ethical overtones is apparent in issues relating to gender. Genevieve Lloyd (1984) makes the point that most major schools of philosophy raise reason as the distinguishing mark of the human and associate reason with the work of men. Emotionality is then subhuman and associated with women. Inge K. Broverman, Susan R. Vogel, Donald M. Broverman, Frank E. Clarkson, and Paul S. Rosenkrantz (1972) demonstrated that such thinking is not limited to philosophers but is evident in mental health professionals as well. In their study, healthy adults and healthy males were described as rational, independent, and aggressive, while females were described as emotional, dependent, and passive.

Mechanism. The core metaphor of mechanism is a machine, for example, a lever (Pepper 1944). The lever operates within a causal structure implicit in nature. Experimentation reveals the universal law that governs the movement and arrangements of the parts of the lever. Moreover, this law can be specified in a quantitative way. Proponents of mechanism have included John Locke ([1960] 1964), who suggested that what can be said of nature can also be said of human history and consciousness. Human nature is lawful, and personal identity is sameness over time. For the political theorist Karl Marx, personal and familial identity is determined by objective economic processes. In psychological theories, the mechanistic metaphor is apparent in B. F. Skinner's behaviorism, in information-processing models of thought, in the hydraulic images of the psyche in classical psychoanalytic thought, and in the medical-model approaches to illness and therapy.

Strategic family therapists (Fisch, Weakland, and Segal 1986; Haley 1976; Madanes 1981, 1984) build on the mechanistic metaphor. Goal-oriented, these therapists focus on techniques of creating change in families. Madanes, for example, reframed a bulimic woman's behavior as throwing away food and instructed her to throw away five dollars' worth of food each day. For strategic family therapists, prescribing the symptomatic behavior is acceptable if it is effective. And the history of the family is not particularly important for the therapy.

Workability is the test of ethics from a mechanist's point of view. In strategic family therapy, the implicit ethic is the predicted power of a formula to produce the desired results. Out of the mechanistic metaphor comes the assumption that what produces the desired change is what *should* be done. While such a model clearly has heuristic value in understanding human thought processes, it also reinforces a linear problem-solving mentality, which flourishes in a technological culture. Technical rationality tends to be linear and instrumental (Kvale 1973). Technology that is built on scientific images, constructs, or models tends to be pragmatic and means oriented, as Jacques Ellul (1964) has clearly pointed out.

The naturalist ethic implicit in the behavior and strategic therapists is subject to critique, as is any other proposed ethical system (Browning 1988b). Alastyre MacIntyre (1981) in his book *After Virtue* comments that therapists in a technological society are incapable of ethical reflection since they assume that their fundamental therapeutic task is to efficiently adapt individuals to a given culture. The ends are assumed; only the means need to be selected and manipulated. Ethical assumptions and prescriptions are masked by the family therapist's commitment to a mechanistic orientation, which is assumed to be ethically neutral.

When human nature is assumed to be a reflection of nature, the theory that emerges may be an ideological justification of the way things already are. Nature language is one way of justifying the ethic of an earlier era now no longer socially assumed (see MacIntyre 1981). Nathan Ackerman (1958), for example, assumed that differences between men and women are a function of nature. Individuals who use nature language of gender differences usually assume it is "natural" for women to be submissive. If pragmatic symptom removal is the goal of therapy, what would preclude making women more submissive to men in order to remove the objectionable symptom?

Contextualism. The core metaphor of contextualism is the historic event, not the past event but the one alive in the present (Pepper 1944). For example, consider the past act of placing a period and the present "life" of that act in the following sentence, "A period will be placed at the end of this sentence." The focus is on acts, their interconnections, and changing patterns. The quality of an event is its intuited whole, and the whole is more than the sum of its parts. This is radically different from the unchangeable ideas of formism and the space-time structure of mechanism. For the contextualist, the order one finds in nature is perceived as a threat to human creativity and spontaneity. Indeed, novelty and change are so prevalent that generalization is extremely difficult.

The contextualistic metaphor is the one most sensitive to the dramatic and historic self. Each person is an actor, and the world is a stage. Since a preexisting order is rejected, there is no preordained script. Instead of chains, we have opportunity. Whether we like it or not, we are "thrown" into a world without meaning. In the act of choosing, however, we create meaning and order. We can freely choose goals, select means, and judge the consequences. Since we are self-aware and self-reflexive beings, the expectations of others need not determine our choices. We are experiencing, feeling persons with natural impulses that must be respected. What results from action and choice is entirely unique. We experience first and reflect second.

The ethic of the contextualistic metaphor is the imperative to individuate, to be responsible for one's own actions. Virtually all family therapists emphasize the importance of separateness in family systems. Probably one of the most articulate proponents of the importance of differentiation, Bowen (1978) holds that the lack of differentiation leads to excess in seeking of approval and love, in relatedness, and in "being-for-others." Though, for Bowen, differentiation is not to be confused with individualism, descriptions of the ideal differentiated individual consists of words and phrases such as "autonomy," "goal-directed," "intellectual," and "being-for-self." Bowen's model reinforces the division of male individualism and female relatedness, with the former characteristic viewed as favorable and the latter as pejorative.

Carl Whitaker (1989) is another family therapist who, in part, embraces the contextualistic approach and its implicit ethic. For him, the pathological family is a family that acts "crazy," is massively inhibited. "Craziness" is measured by the degree to which creative, nonrational impulsiveness in the family is integrated with psychosocial adaptability. Whitaker's goal in therapy is to develop family belongingness and individual freedom and to increase the creativity (craziness) of the family and the individual members. Clearly, his goal is not social adaptation. The healthy family, according to Whitaker, allows a flexible distribution of power and grants freedom of choice to each member in the family. It has an available "as if" structure, which permits individual members to take on different roles. Roles are a result of interaction, not dictation, and are defined by a range of conditions: the past, the present, the future, the culture, and family demands. Problems are solved by marshaling customs, myths, family rules, hopes, taboos, and facts.

The contextualistic metaphor seems most appropriate for the self when the context is social or familial oppression: for the adolescent unable to develop autonomy, for the woman whose roles are rigidly defined by men, and for the individual who is very dependent on others for self-definition. However, given the individualism in American society (Bellah et al. 1985), this metaphor prescribes a remedy that may exacerbate the existing problem, namely, individualism. One must wonder whether the emphasis on differentiation is truly a response to enmeshed families or whether it reflects a more general cultural commitment to individualism.

Organicism. The core metaphor in organicism is the dynamic, changing organism. In organicism every actual event in the world is a concealed organic process. The organicist notes the steps in the organic process and the principal features in the ideal structure achieved or realized, which is elaborated in Pepper's definition: "the specific categories are: (1) fragments of experience which appear with (2) nexuses or connections or implications, which spontaneously lead as a result of the aggravation of (3) contradictions, gaps, opposition, or counteractions to resolution in (4) an organic whole, which is found to have been (5) implicit in the fragments, and to (6) transcend the previous contradictions by means of a coherent totality, which (7) economizes, saves, preserves all the original fragments of experience without any loss" (1944, 283).

The process of further integration is not smooth, for fragments conflict with other fragments, creating contradiction. Each higher integration incorporates earlier stages. Resolution, the end product which is always an integration of conflicting fragments, is one absolutely concrete, coherent, organic whole. For the organicist, progress is defined as movement in the direction of greater inclusiveness, determinateness, and organicity. The system is organic if every element implies every other element or if a change in one element would alter every other element. Though this description may be an ideal, the organicist envisages a continuous bridge from partial evidence to ultimate fact and is dogmatic about the inherent contradictoriness of all experience. Out of the contradictoriness of all partial facts springs the ethical assumption implicit in the organic metaphor: there is evidence for the coherence of the ultimate and this coherence is the norm for physical, psychological, and social reality.

The structural/systemic approach to understanding the family is a logical and ethical elaboration of the organic metaphor. In this perspective the family is seen as a whole rather than merely a sum of its parts (see Hoffman 1981; Minuchin and Fishman 1981; Minuchin, Rosman, and Baker 1978). At first, there are only individuals in a family and no coherence. But all families change, positively or negatively, toward greater integration. Individual behavior becomes meaningful when it is brought into a coherent system of beliefs and feelings and connected with other behaviors in the family story.

Some family theorists argue that systems theory is only descriptive, not prescriptive. But is systems theory indeed that ethically neutral, or is there a "systems ethics"? Implicit in the organic metaphor is an ethic that is relational, flexible, and evolutionary. Its fundamental value is connectedness, and it encourages what moves toward integration and away from individualism. From the way systems therapists now conduct therapy, it appears there are specific ethical mandates implicit in systems theory. For example, in healthy systems (a) boundaries should not be rigid but flexible, (b) individual responses should be adaptable to external change, (c) systems and subsystems should be separated in their functions, and (d) subsystems should be connected through communication.

Those who question the ethic implicit in systems theory suggest that what is needed is a more historical perspective on the family, since systems theory tends to be historically neutral and devoid of historical content. Regarding systems theory, Kerrie James and Deborah McIntyre offer the following critique:

> The argument is that while it can provide a useful view of the interrelationships between elements of a system, it can make no comment on the nature of the system itself. In the context of this discussion, systems theory must accept existing social structure. It can describe their interactions; it cannot comment on, or question the validity and desirability of, the structures themselves. In this way, moral, social, and political questions are collapsed into technical issues requiring technological intervention. (1983, 127)

Deborah A. Luepnitz, in her evaluation of systems theory, says that "functionalists can explain how parts of a system fit together, but they are hard-pressed to explain how parts could be fundamentally at odds with one another" (1988, 65). Moreover, conflict or change is seen in terms of some larger social need.

Functionalism and systems theory can evaluate how efficiently parts are functioning relative to a larger system. But what happens when the larger whole is not questioned? It might result in a model that is politically conservative. Consider this argument by Luepnitz:

> A feminist family therapy cannot rest on functionalist principles; it must begin with a critical and historical understanding of the family. It also requires non-functionalist language. I have argued elsewhere that to speak of families' pain, darkness and pleasure in terms of "functional effectiveness" and "dysfunction" dehumanizes our work. . . . Such language can be used to normalize any reciprocal behavior pattern in a family or group, from the most benign forms of cooperation to the most cynical forms of dominance and submission. (1988, 67)

Such a critique of the implicit ethic of systems theory indicates that the ethical metaphor is too limited. The abstract structural theories blur the impact of oppressive roles assigned to women, the critical role of a family's ethnic history, and the importance of the religious story that shapes a family.

Metaphors and Moral Language. The four metaphors (formism, mechanism, contextualism, and organicism) operate in different theoretical orientations to provide a set of practices to guide therapeutic interventions. These interventions, the stuff of family therapy, are implicitly ethical in nature. Conversation, theoretical or ethical, between proponents of the approaches varies from professional tolerance to blatant acrimony. It would appear that family therapists reflect a present fragmentation of moral languages.

MacIntyre has challenged the assumption that there is any consensus on the meaning of moral terms in modernity. He states: "What we possess . . . are the fragments of a conceptual scheme, parts which now lack those contexts from which their significance derived. We possess indeed simulacra of morality, we continue to use many of the key expressions. But we have—very largely, if not entirely—lost our comprehension, both theoretical

and practical, of morality" (1981, 5). MacIntyre suggests that
what we need is not further philosophical systematization of the
fragments but historical analysis. Our use of parts of moral
schemas without the original social context in which they were
meaningful has given rise to the babel of tongues current in
moral discourse. Given the disarray of moral theory, we have no
objective way of weighing one moral claim against another. And,
without a historical context for moral claims, these claims are
presented in an impersonal, abstract mode.

While Jeffrey Stout agrees that there is a plurality of moral
languages, he is less pessimistic than MacIntyre about the consequences:

> The languages of morals in our discourse are many, and they
> have remarkably diverse historical origins, but they do not float
> in free air, and their name is not chaos. They are embedded in
> specific social practices and institutions—religious, political,
> artistic, scientific, athletic, economic, and so on. We need many
> different moral concepts because there are many different lin-
> guistic threads woven into any fabric of practices and institu-
> tions as rich as ours. It is a motley; not a building in need of a
> new foundation but a coat of many colors, one constantly in need
> of mending and patching, sometimes even recutting and
> restyling. (1988, 291–92)

In agreement with Stout's more positive reframing of the situation from chaos to diversity, I endorse the use of many languages to facilitate healing. Hence, I would add *therapy* to his
list of specific social practices and institutions in which moral
languages are embedded.

Stout's proposed response to the plurality of moral languages is that we stitch the fragments together as is needed for
a given situation. However, I am less confident than he that
moral *bricolage* (the selective retrieval and eclectic reconfigu-
ration of fragments of traditional moral language in solving the
problems at hand) alone is the solution to the diversity. Some
additional resources are needed. Indeed, Stout's proposal begs
the question of what shapes the process of bricolage. How does
the contemporary family therapist select metaphors, let alone
fill them with moral content? To be sure, it is a process that is
shaped in part by the situation at hand; however, I would suggest that it is the normative story of the therapist that shapes

the process of selection and retrieval of metaphors. For me, that story is the story and practice I learned from the reading of the biblical text, the ethical praxis of my religious community, and the example of Christians throughout history. For me, it is the story of the reign of God that informs this process of moral bricolage. In Jesus' words, "Therefore every scribe who has been trained for the kingdom of heaven is like the master of a household who brings out of his treasure what is new and what is old" (Matt. 13:52 NRSV).

Ethical Models of Family within Culture

Not only do implicit metaphors shape the ethical responses of family therapists, particular models of the family, which are embedded in culture, also shape them. Neither families nor family therapists function in a historical vacuum (Bernal and Ysern 1986; Dueck 1985); neither families nor therapists are disembodied systems or parts of systems floating in atemporal space. Both are shaped by and shape the social and historical settings in which they exist. Contained within the social context are not only the aforementioned metaphors but also models of what the family is and should be. These models, which are elaborated metaphors (Barbour 1974), indicate more specifically the contours of the family implicated by the image.

The social context of the family today is modernity (Lasch 1978; Poster 1978; Shorter 1975; Skolnick and Skolnick 1989). Two major models of the family coexist in this milieu. Though both models shape the family therapist, one is usually rejected. One model flourishes in politically conservative groups, in some religious communities, and in ethnic populations. The other prospers in more politically liberal groups and in families thoroughly socialized into the values of modernity. Each model specifies the roles to be played or negotiated, the ideal of a healthy family, the family's relationship to society, and so on. The models, like the metaphors, are both descriptive and prescriptive.

Family therapy is an ethical enterprise. Failure to take seriously family therapy's social context raises an ethical issue. Social amnesia results in a covert imposition of values, which is as serious as overt imposition. Feminists have been most articulate regarding their concern that family therapy socialized families into the values of the dominant culture (Hare-Mustin 1978, 1987). Not surprisingly, concern has also been raised by ethnic and religious families who sense they are being socialized into values alien to their convictions. Determining the culture to which families should adapt is an ethical issue. Family therapy is also fundamentally political, in that family therapists are members of a particular culture. Insofar as therapists participate in a process of socializing families into a specific cultural milieu, they are ethical agents. Clifford Geertz (1973) has suggested that culture be defined as religion. If culture is so defined, then value neutrality is a myth modernists use to hide their particularity. Specifically, culture reinforces a differential allocation of power, status, privilege, and access to resources on the basis of gender.

Premodern and Modern Family Models. Family therapists implicitly accept one cultural model or a combination of models. The ethical nature of their work arises from the ethical nature of the family models, which can be classified into two groups: premodern (or traditional) and modern. A fundamental shift has taken place in the family as life-styles changed from being agricultural, rural, and conservative to industrial, urban, and liberal. In traditional societies, the individual is assumed to be an integral part of the community. The harmony of the whole is a critical issue in solving disputes. The needs of the family are assumed to overrule the needs of the individual. Whereas in traditional societies the family is absolute, in modern societies it is not taken seriously enough. In liberal societies, the individual is viewed as needing to be released from oppressive communities. Self-realization is the goal. Society and family are there for the sake of individual development. There is no ethic of sacrifice for another generation.

In conservative societies, there are ties with communities outside of the family: inviting friends over (the Sunday noon meal) or being involved in local functions. The needs of the larger community are important, but in conservative societies the needs of children may go unattended. Urban societies encourage few ties to the larger community, which results in what has been referred to as the "domestication" of the family. The individual is an extension of the family. The family becomes ingrown; emotions intensify. All energy is consumed in simply meeting the everyday needs of the immediate family. The traditional family is surrounded by several generations of its members as well as the larger community. Children live nearby after marriage, and maintaining contact with family members is seen as an obligation. The unfortunate and the old are housed and cared for. Disabled children are absorbed into the fabric of community life. Children born out of wedlock are often taken in by the grandparents, as is done in some Afro-American communities. Remember, however, that the very cohesion which makes becoming a member possible creates incredible pain when one is excluded. And traditional communities have not always cared for those who deviate. In modern societies, the extended family is gone. The nuclear family lives in housing tracts, not neighborhoods. The nuclear family, whose size has been reduced to two children, physically moves away from the parent family. As a result, the family feels isolated, alone. Also reduced is any sense of responsibility for kin.

In traditional societies, parenting is the responsibility of the entire community. There are a great number of significant role models, and the wisdom of the larger community is brought to bear on a problem. At the same time, it is difficult to try alternatives. There are ways in which parents have handled stress before, whether that stress is caused by a disobedient adolescent or a disabled child; hence, some folk wisdom might apply. But the child in the traditional family took a subordinate position to survival of the community. Modernity assumes that the nuclear family has all the skills that are necessary to take care of the next generation. Children in modernity are an extension of the biological parents, not the community. The individual family relies on its own history of experience with the children in parenting; hence, families experience a sense of helplessness. Furthermore, in modernity it is assumed that the center of emotional life is the family. Parents hang on to the children for emotional support and tend to be overprotective of them.

In traditional societies, the family is the key agent for socializing children into the ideals of the community. Education comes by working together. The family is an economic unit, and children are an economic asset. Each family member can make a contribution or carry those who cannot, thus creating a sense of unity. In the urban setting, the home is a hotel, where people eat and sleep. Parents work away from home; children are educated in public institutions. Entertainment occurs at convention centers or gyms or theaters. For the modern family, children are a financial liability.

Authority in conservative settings is accepted as legitimate and exercised in favor of the community's ideals. At its best, authority is legitimated by truth; however, often it is hierarchical, based on status and family. Many windows to the external world are open to the traditional family. If the community is aware of a family problem, there are external pressures to resolve it. In fact, community leaders are likely to directly address the problem. Not only is the modern family separate from the community, it is autonomous. The church or community does not meddle in the life of the family. A couple decides the number of children they will have, the mode of birth control, and the appropriateness of having an abortion or taking the risk of bearing a disabled child. Where there is authority, it is based not on status but on friendship. Parents are companions. Personal freedom and choice are highly valued. The peer group may be a more powerful shaper of attitudes than the family. Egalitarian relationships are assumed. Significantly lost are the language of obedience and a sense of control. Accountable only to its own norms, the modern family is autonomous, makes its own decisions, and indulges in self-pity when failure occurs.

Family Models and Ethics. How do family models relate to ethics? Let's consider a few of the ways. A given family therapist may identify with only one of the family models. For the therapist, one may be normative, the standard by which a family in therapy is measured. Take the issue of authority. Some family therapists accept and some reject the more traditional model. Ackerman, for example, laments the loss of the authority of the father. He states that the father "has been stripped of all semblance of arbitrary authority in the family members, whether wife or child. . . . Wife and child deferred to his superior wisdom. He exercised his authority firmly but fairly. His discipline was strict but not abusive. . . . Sometimes he became the tyrant; if so, in the end he suffered for the abuse of his power. Echoes of this older image persist, but they have grown dim" (1958, 179). Many family therapists would take a modern democratic approach to the role of the father in which author-ity emerges from conversation and is shared with the spouse.

The family therapist is one of many agents who socialize the family into the values of a particular society. When the values of a particular subculture (e.g., women, minorities, or religious groups) deviate from the values of society, a socially unaware family therapist becomes an agent of oppressive socialization of sexism, white culture, or secularism. A family therapist may assume that modernity as we know it is an appropriate ethical context for therapy or that culture is simply an ethically neu-tral collage of customs. On the contrary, modernity is both descriptive and prescriptive (Geertz 1973). The family thera-pist may assume that modernity as we know it is an appropri-ate ethical context for therapy or that culture is simply an eth-ically neutral collage of customs.

If culture is the normative context of the family and the fam-ily therapist, family therapy not surprisingly reflects the val-ues, methods, and paradoxes of modernity and postmodernity. It is not from culture in general that family therapy emerges, but rather from a particular culture, namely, modernity. This culture is variously described as postindustrial, technological, secular, egalitarian, individualistic, and scientific. Socialization into the values of modernity is a consequence of education and professional training. Not surprisingly, the contemporary fam-ily therapist appears profoundly modern. Socialization into the values of modernity shapes the way therapists view the pre-modern family and the degree to which it should be modern. Which cultural vision shapes the family therapist's view of the ideal family is indeed an ethical issue.

The feminist critique of our culture points to another way in which family models relate to ethics. With their vision of a more egalitarian culture, feminists plead for a more historical reading of the family (Braverman 1987; McGoldrick, Anderson, and Walsh 1989). There is, they argue, a long history of pater-nalism, which affects the balance of power in families, not to mention the mental health of female family members (Hafner 1986). Nancy Chodorow has cogently argued that the contem-porary form of the family, with father absent and mother over-involved in the children's lives, is a function of the economic context. She states: "Women's mothering in the isolated nuclear family of contemporary capitalist society creates specific personality characteristics in men that reproduce both an ideology and psychodynamic of male superiority and submission to the requirements of production. It prepares men for participation in male-dominated family and society, for their lesser emotional participation in family life, and for their participation in the capitalist world of work" (1978, 180).

Luepnitz has shown that the labeling of families as adequate or functional is also a matter of ethics. For evidence, she points to the classic Timberlawn study of families (Lewis et al. 1976). In the adequate families (in comparison with dysfunctional and optimal ones), the wives were overwhelmed with responsibility, were overweight, suffered from psychosomatic illness, and were sexually dissatisfied. The husbands in the adequate group were described as functioning well. Thus, according to the study, an adequate family is one in which the husband is functioning well and the wife is functioning marginally. Luepnitz concludes that "the question of what one decides to term *adequate* or *functional* and what one decides is instead a serious social problem is a question of values or ideology. And indeed the most transformative insight that a feminist perspective can offer family therapists is the realization that ideas do not fall from the sky; they are artifacts constructed by people whose thinking is never ideologically impartial" (1988, 11).

Culture does indeed provide models for the ideal family, and family therapists are part of a particular culture. Most assuredly, it is an ethical issue when therapists assume one family model is normative.

Implicit Ethical Paradigms in Family Therapy

Any number of ethical paradigms could be chosen to illustrate how moral-ethical principles can be used to guide family therapy. The one I have chosen is the enlightenment paradigm of Ivan Boszormenyi-Nagy. Boszormenyi-Nagy and his colleagues (Boszormenyi-Nagy and Krasner 1986; Boszormenyi-Nagy and Spark 1973; Boszormenyi-Nagy and Ulrich 1981) have deliberately introduced moral and ethical language into their concept of the family and into their interventions with families. Family therapy, they state, must be ethically concerned and contractually responsible. As should be quite clear by now, family therapy simply cannot get away from ethics, for ethical issues of fairness permeate our daily lives and relationships, not just the Old and New Testaments. But what about Boszormenyi-Nagy's claim that therapy must be contractually responsible? The concept is not as foreign as one might think. Any person who says "The only one you owe anything is yourself" or "You owe it to your parents to at least call them once in a while" is using a contractual metaphor to describe relationships.

Boszormenyi-Nagy and his associates propose that family therapy should deal with ethical notions of loyalty, ledgers, and legacies in relationships. Health in families is built on the loyalty commitments of parents to children, on a balance of payments between spouses and children, and on the existence of moderate expectations on future generations. Together these ethical notions, they argue, constitute a relational ethic of right and wrong. Family therapy is then a matter of rebuilding relationships.

Loyalty. Boszormenyi-Nagy and his associates assume that the desire for trustworthy relationships is the foundation of healing. While our common rootedness creates an obligation and a legacy, relationships are built on trust and loyalty. Loyalty is "a preferential attachment to relational partners who are entitled to a priority of 'bonding'" (Boszormenyi-Nagy and Krasner 1986, 418; see also the chapter by Krasner and Joyce in this volume). The goals of this model of therapy involve the discovery of resources of trustworthiness: rejunctive (i.e., relationship enhancing) action, relational integrity, and a balanced ledger. The capacity for affection and intimacy cannot be preserved unless there is an honest commitment to balance the ledger. Rejunctive efforts preserve loyalty and exonerate the previous generation (forgive the debt). Families can find more appropriate ways of paying debts than by incurring more debts in the present generation. The family therapist seeks to determine the state of the balance in the ledger and to develop a commitment to fairness. Each family member's perspective is considered, accountability is encouraged, and individuals are empowered to contribute to another person's account. The family therapist seeks to loosen invisible loyalties and legacies to previous generations. Fairness demands that the therapist exhibit multidirectional partiality to each member of the family.

Ledger. In contextual family therapy, ethics is defined as a balance of fairness between people. Boszormenyi-Nagy and David N. Ulrich state that "'ethics' carries no implication of a specific set of moral priorities or criteria of right vs. wrong. It is concerned with the balance of equitable fairness between people . . . the long-term preservation of an oscillating balance among family members, whereby the basic interests of each are taken into account by the others" (1981, 160). The ledger indicates the psychological sense of entitlement and indebtedness. Merit in the ledger is accumulated by contribution to the welfare of others. Trust in relationships is a function of the long-term status of credits and debits.

Dysfunctional families are disjunctive in nature in that they move away from relatedness. When fairness is no longer a concern in relationships and when one feels one cannot collect on a debt, stagnation, loss of intimacy, and a feeling of exploitation occur. There is also the possibility of corruption and intentional unfairness in the family.

Legacy. Legacy is the state of the ledger at the time of birth and the state of expectation projected on the next generation. Not statements of pleasure and pain, legacy expectations are ethical imperatives: "I ought to do this." The "oughtness" emerges out of having simply been born (loyalty) and having to pay a debt to previous generations and provide credit for subsequent generations (ledger).

No one member of the family can judge whether there is a balance of debits and credits in the family ledger across generations. The payment of debts can be made only to the person to whom one is in debt, in contrast to symbolic repayment to the therapist. Repayment occurs only in the way one has been taught to repay, for example, the beaten child becomes the child-beating parent. Parents are responsible for parenting, for taking the child's welfare into consideration, thereby developing merit. Children repay by being loyal and trusting.

Previous generations may pass on indebtedness if they assume the next generation must succeed where the previous ones failed. Parents who abuse their children pay a debt for a long time. They are drawing on an empty account, since children cannot parent the parents. Children may be so mystified that they are never able to view the ledger and see the balance of payments to previous generations. Parents may assume that the debt to grandparents is endless, and so they have no resources for the next generation. Parents may split the loyalty of children to each parent and thus make payment into the family ledger difficult. Pathology is viewed as an attempt to balance the ledger in inappropriate ways (e.g., anorexia, shoplifting, and so on). Sometimes parents keep records (balance the checkbook) in the same way their parents did. A father may treat a son in the same way that grandfather treated his son, out of loyalty to the grandfather. This behavior avoids dealing with the balance of accounts in the present family. If there is a debt in the ledger, children may seek to make it up, leading to parentification. When an individual cannot collect a debt from the original debtor, substitutes are found. When there is an imbalance in the ledger, symptoms emerge. The nuclear family then lives in a state of isolation and debt.

According to Boszormenyi-Nagy and his associates, ethical family therapists explore where there is loyalty and trust in relationships and also where there is parentification, exploitation, and corruption. Ethical family therapists encourage open negotiation on ledger matters. For the family to make adjustments so the balance of payments is equal in the long run is the goal of therapy. Parents pay out more while offspring are young, and children pay out more as their parents grow older and have more needs. Then exploitation is stopped. Since there is trust, autonomy can emerge. There is no hidden ledger of unpaid debts that keeps some members in bondage to others. Loyalties are free to change as the life cycle changes.

The Enlightenment Paradigm. Boszormenyi-Nagy and his colleagues are explicit about therapy's being an ethical process. Moreover, the ethic they espouse is in many ways consistent with a Judeo-Christian ethic. At the root of Boszormenyi-Nagy's contextual family therapy approach to ethics is an "enlightenment." Exhibiting the influence of Immanuel Kant, John Stuart Mill, Jean-Jacques Rousseau, and Jeremy Bentham (Robinson 1976), the enlightenment paradigm begins with the assumption that ethics is by nature universal rather than particular and that individual ethical agents intuitively know the meaning of ethical language (e.g., justice and fairness). Ethics is a matter of following moral principles that will reestablish harmony in the family. Moral principles are, however, abridgments of tradition (Stout 1988). For those who know and accept the tradition, the principles are useful. Don Browning (1976, 1988a) has repeatedly raised the question of the content of moral language and how that moral content is determined. The moral content of moral language is provided by a particular tradition. In the approach of Boszormenyi-Nagy and his colleagues, the moral content comes from both religious sources (Buber 1958) and secular ones (Sullivan 1947).

In the past two decades, the universalist model has come under increasing criticism by ethicists such as Alastyre MacIntyre (1981), Jeffrey Stout (1988), and Stanley Hauerwas (1974, 1977, 1981, 1983). Stout refers to the ethical language used in the model as moral Esperanto, an attempt to create a universal ethical language. Hauerwas challenges the universalist assumption: "All ethical reflection occurs relative to a particular time and place. Not only do ethical problems change from one time to the next, but the very nature and structure of ethics is determined by the particularities of a community's history and convictions" (1983, 1). MacIntyre indicates that in classical (Greco-Roman) societies morality was characterized by particularity and accountability. There was no desire to aspire to universality. From these societies, he suggests, we need to learn that "all morality is always to some degree tied to the socially local and particular and that the aspirations of the morality of modernity to a universality freed from all particularity is an illusion" and that "there is no way to possess the virtues except as part of a tradition in which we inherit them and our understanding of them from a series of predecessors in which series heroic societies hold first place" (1981, 119).

As is usually the case, a universalist model of ethics usually presumes some form of particularity. The model presented by the contextualists is uniquely Western. The implicit narrative shaping the ethic is the capitalist story with its emphasis on contracts, its focus on balance in ledgers, and its concern with economic fairness. While to use the language of contracts familiar to Americans may be a strategic move therapeutically, one wonders how limiting it is ethically and why the language of contracts was selected over the language of, say, consequentialism.

Boszormenyi-Nagy and his colleagues have appropriately introduced the language of ethics into their approach to family therapy. This school of therapy is one of the few that addresses the issue of justice. But from this issue springs a valid question: "Whose version of justice?" In the last section of this chapter, I explore how religious particularity might address this issue of ethics—justice—in therapy. Self-consciously confessional, the section is written without an attempt to address the moral sensibilities of all possible clients and family therapists. The narrative emerges out of my experience as one who grew up in an Anabaptist-Mennonite community.

The Reign of God as the Narrative and Ethical Context of Family Therapy

The reign of God as it was announced and described by Jesus is the narrative context for the metaphors, models, and paradigms that shape my work with families (Dueck 1987a, 1987b, 1987c, 1989a, 1989b). Much of what I have written heretofore about specific metaphors, models, and paradigms as ethical dimensions of therapy may be helpful if the particularity of the reign of God is the point of departure. What shapes the appropriateness of particular metaphors or models for therapy is determined by my sense of their consistency with the plot, the subthemes, and the characters of the *story* of the reign of God.

We are called to give the reign of God highest priority (Matt. 6:33). This suggests that the reign of God has a higher ethical priority than the family's construal of itself or the particular metaphor a family therapist finds personally satisfying. It is the reign of God as an emerging culture that serves as the basis for assessing the various models of culture and family. For me, the reign of God is the test of the principles that Boszormenyi-Nagy and his colleagues suggest as normative for therapy.

As the context for the ethical mandate to the family, the reign of God is an ethical vision that gives meaning and direction to family life. The family has a story to tell, a sense of mission and purpose beyond its own perpetuation. The family does not create a unique story all its own, but its story is a part of and an extension of the story of God's reign in the world. As does any other community, the family has rituals and symbols that express its ethical vision. The family that places its story in the context of the narrative of God's reign participates as members in the rituals of servanthood (footwashing), of sorrow (Good Friday), of hope (Easter), of new life (Christmas), of membership (baptism), and of commitment (worship). To the extent a family is actively involved in these rituals, it immerses itself in a larger story.

The reign of God, with the church as a sign of its presence, is the normative context of the family. The church is then the family's new home. Not simply a collection of individuals or of families, the church is called to be a community in which individuals and families obtain their nourishment and identity (Bellah 1987). The church is a community that provides to the family an alternative context to the one provided by fragmented modern society (Coles 1987).

Metaphors and the Reign of God

Each of the four metaphors that shape Western metaphysics and ethics—formism, mechanism, contextualism, and organicism—is a reflection of both ancient and modern experience. Formists focus on the experience of similarity and difference and the construction of a plan. Mechanists highlight the experience of order in nature and human inventions. The contextualists accent human action, while the organicists emphasize relatedness. One can hardly deny the validity of the experiences these metaphors describe. Though one can make a case for the dualism of mind and body in experience as a mechanist, it is not a basis of ethical judgment in the New Testament.

There is nothing in the story of the reign of God that denies that *what* the metaphors describe is a part of human experience. However, Jesus simply does not begin with a metaphor or metaphysic, deduce an ethic, and then apply it to all human experience. To choose the reign of God epistemologically at the outset means that metaphors from human experience cannot function autonomously as the source of metaphors for our interventions and understanding of families. The primary metaphors in the New Testament's account of the reign of God begin with who God is in relationship to humankind, not with ethical or metaphysical metaphors.

Models and the Reign of God

The family therapist borrows models of the family from culture, a historical situation which is no different for the therapist with Judeo-Christian beliefs. However, my vision for the ethical society/culture is the reign of God. The reign Jesus promises and inaugurates is a social, historical community (Borg 1984, 1988; Yoder 1972), which is rooted in the movement that began with the exodus and continues today. In its historical manifestation, the community is a group of persons who take the values of the reign of God as the point of departure but who are subject to the same social forces that the contemporary family and family therapist experience.

A commitment to the reign of God as the point of departure does not erase the shift from preindustrial to postmodern society. Nor does the commitment automatically bless or romanticize the agrarian past as the golden age or the egalitarian modern family as the ethical ideal. However, such a commitment does reject hierarchicalism, for as Jesus reminds us, "You know that the rulers of the Gentiles lord it over them. . . . Not so with you" (Matt. 20:25–26 NIV). For me, it is a social vision of the reign of God that makes sexual oppression intolerable. In his relationships to women, Jesus demonstrated that he valued women first as human, capable of intellectual and emotional exchange.

A commitment to the reign of God as the norm relativizes the family's claim to final authority. When the disciples went to Jesus informing him that his mother and family were waiting outside to see him, Jesus responded with a question and a statement: "'Who is my mother, and who are my brothers?' Pointing to his disciples, he said, 'Here are my mother and my brothers. For whoever does the will of my Father in heaven is my brother and sister and mother'" (Matt. 12:48–50 NIV). In other words, while the social context of the family is the current historical setting (e.g., Roman or capitalist), the ethical context of the family is the reign of God. The story of the reign of God relativizes the family's autonomy, for the family is accountable to a larger social vision. The reign-of-God narrative even relativizes the power of blood. Whereas the human family is built on the power of kinship, the reign of God transcends the bonds of kin.

The reign of God is a social movement that clashes with contemporary individualism and its impact on the family. The values of the reign of God include differentiation and connection. The church as a sign of the kingdom recognizes the dignity of the individual and the importance of commitment to the whole. This does not mean, however, that individual identity is lost in the church. Though there is no place for narcissism in this setting, the individual has dignity and is encouraged to grow and develop. The reign of God also points to community, and traditionally churches have provided such connectedness. Members may work together, pray together, live near each other, teach Sunday school together, and have picnics together. But a commitment to the reign of God does not mean a fusion of families in the people of God any more than being a member of a family presumes enmeshment.

Paradigms and the Reign of God

Out of the narrative of the reign of God emerges the assumption that ethics is political, communal, and historical. The reign of God is a particular story, and it has particular characteristics. The church as a community of individuals and families is called to incarnate a particular set of values. The therapist who self-consciously seeks to incarnate the values of the reign of God in personal life and in therapy makes the narrative of God's reign the starting point for a social theory of the good society in which the family is embedded. When there is no normative vision of society, then existing mores and values of the host culture (e.g., those of the capitalist story) fill in.

I have only begun the process of translating the implications of the story of the reign of God for specific aspects of family therapy. For the sake of personal integrity, the task of "integrating" Christianity and psychology is for me less a matter of finding a theoretical average between the two and more a matter of beginning with my story and drawing out the implications. In the words of Jeffrey Stout, "moral philosophy is not practiced from the vantage point of omniscience, above history. It begins, for any of us, at some particular site, where some moral languages are in use. . . . [Moral philosophy] is a kind of reflexive ethnography. It begins at home, with languages in use, and then reaches out to other possibilities, accessible from its particular historical position" (1988, 72). I have attempted to begin the process Stout describes. The fragments of moral languages available in the public sphere are useful insofar as they can be incorporated into and are consistent with the particular story of a particular therapist. Though the particular story should not be universally imposed on clients by the therapist, it should influence the content of the metaphors, models, and paradigms that shape the therapeutic process.

References

Ackerman, N. 1958. *The psychodynamics of family life*. New York: Basic.

Augsburger, D. 1989. *Hope for the family*. Ventura, Calif.: Regal.

Bagarozzi, D. A., and S. A. Anderson. 1988. *Personal, marital, and family myths: Theoretical formulations and clinical strategies*. New York: Norton.

Barbour, I. G. 1974. *Myths, models, and paradigms*. New York: Harper and Row.

Bellah, R. 1987. The church as the context for the family. *New Oxford Review* 54:6–13.

Bellah, R., R. Madsen, W. Sullivan, A. Swidler, and S. Tipton. 1985. *Habits of the heart: Individualism and commitment in American life*. Berkeley and Los Angeles: University of California Press.

Bernal, G., and E. Ysern. 1986. Family therapy and ideology. *Journal of Marital and Family Therapy* 12:129–35.

Borg, M. 1984. *Conflict, holiness, and politics in the teachings of Jesus*. Toronto: E. Mellen.

———. 1988. *Jesus: A new vision*. San Francisco: Harper and Row.

Boszormenyi-Nagy, I., and B. R. Krasner. 1986. *Between give and take: A clinical guide to contextual therapy*. New York: Brunner/Mazel.

Boszormenyi-Nagy, I., and D. N. Ulrich. 1981. Contextual family therapy. In *Handbook of family therapy*, ed. A. S. Gurman and D. P. Kniskern, 159–86. New York: Brunner/Mazel.

Boszormenyi-Nagy, I., and G. M. Spark. 1973. *Invisible loyalties: Reciprocity in intergenerational family therapy*. Hagerstown, Md.: Harper and Row.

Bowen, M. 1978. *Family therapy in clinical practice.* New York: Aronson.

Braverman, L., ed. 1988. *Women, feminism, and family therapy.* New York: Haworth Press.

Broverman, I. K., S. R. Vogel, D. M. Broverman, F. E. Clarkson, and P. S. Rosenkrantz. 1972. Sex-role stereotypes: A current appraisal. *Journal of Social Issues* 8:59–78.

Browning, D. S. 1976. *Moral context of pastoral care.* Philadelphia: Westminster.

———. 1988a. The pastoral counselor as ethicist: What difference do we make? *Journal of Pastoral Care* 42:283–98.

———. 1988b. *Religious thought and the modern psychologies.* Philadelphia: Fortress.

Buber, M. 1970. *I and thou.* Trans. R. Smith. New York: Scribner. Original German edition published 1923.

Chodorow, N. 1978. *The reproduction of mothering: Psychoanalysis and the sociology of gender.* Berkeley and Los Angeles: University of California Press.

Coles, R. 1987. Moral purpose and the family. *Family Therapy Networker* 11:45–52.

Dueck, A. 1985. North American psychology: Gospel of modernity. *Conrad Grebel Review* 3:165–78.

———. 1987a. Ethical contexts of healing: Character and ritual. *Pastoral Psychology* 36:69–83.

———. 1987b. Ethical contexts of healing: Ecclesia and praxis. *Pastoral Psychology* 36:49–62.

———. 1987c. Ethical contexts of healing: Peoplehood and righteousness. *Pastoral Psychology* 35:239–53.

———. 1989a. On living in Athens: Models of relating psychology, church, and culture. *Journal of Psychology and Christianity* 8:5–18.

———. 1989b. Story, community, and ritual: Anabaptist themes and mental health. *Mennonite Quarterly Review* 63:77–91.

Ellul, J. 1964. *The technological society.* New York: Vintage.

Fisch, R., J. H. Weakland, and L. Segal. 1986. *The tactics of change.* San Francisco: Jossey-Bass.

Geertz, C. 1973. *The interpretation of cultures.* New York: Basic.

Green, S. L., and J. C. Hansen. 1989. Ethical dilemmas faced by family therapists. *Journal of Marital and Family Therapy* 15, 2: 149–58.

Hafner, R. J. 1986. *Marriage and mental illness: A sex roles perspective.* New York: Guilford Press.

Haley, J. 1976. *Problem solving therapy.* San Francisco: Jossey-Bass.

Hansen, J. C., and L. L'Abate, eds. 1982. *Values, ethics, legalities, and the family therapist.* Rockville, Md.: Aspen Systems.

Hare-Mustin, R. T. 1978. A feminist approach to family therapy. *Family Process* 17:181–94.

———. 1987. The problem of gender in family therapy. *Family Process* 26:15–27.

Hauerwas, S. 1974. *Vision and virtue: Essays in Christian ethical reflection.* Notre Dame, Ind.: Fides Publishers.

———. 1977. *Truthfulness and tragedy: Further investigations into Christian ethics.* Notre Dame, Ind.: University of Notre Dame Press.

———. 1981. *A community of character: Toward a constructive Christian social ethic.* Notre Dame, Ind.: University of Notre Dame Press.

———. 1983. *The peaceable kingdom: A primer in Christian ethics.* Notre Dame, Ind.: University of Notre Dame Press.

Hoffman, L. 1981. *Foundations of family therapy: A conceptual framework for systems change.* New York: Basic.

Huber, C. H., and L. G. Baruth. 1987. *Ethical, legal, and professional issues in the practice of marriage and family therapy.* Columbus: Merrill.

James, K., and D. McIntyre. 1983. The reproduction of families: The social role of family therapy? *Journal of Marital and Family Therapy* 9:119–29.

Keith-Spiegel, P., and G. P. Koocher. 1985. *Ethics in psychology: Professional standards and cases.* Hillsdale, N.J.: L. Erlbaum Associates.

Kelly, G. A. 1969. *Clinical psychology and personality: The selected papers of George Kelly.* Ed. B. Maher. New York: Wiley.

Kottler, J., and W. H. Van Hoose. 1977. *Ethical and legal issues in counseling and psychotherapy.* San Francisco: Jossey-Bass.

Kvale, S. 1973. The technological paradigm of psychological research. *Journal of Phenomenological Psychology* 3:143–59.

Lasch, C. 1978. *Haven in a heartless world.* New York: Basic.

Lewis, J. M., W. R. Beavers, J. T. Gossett, and V. A. Phillips. 1976. *No single thread: Psychological health in family systems.* New York: Brunner/Mazel.

Lloyd, G. 1984. *The man of reason: "Male" and "female" in Western philosophy*. London: Methuen.

Locke, J. [1690] 1964. *An essay on human understanding*. Reprint. New York: New American Library.

Luepnitz, D. A. 1988. *The family interpreted: Feminist theory in clinical practice*. New York: Basic.

McGoldrick, M., C. M. Anderson, and F. Walsh, eds. 1989. *Women in families: A framework for family therapy*. New York: Norton.

MacIntyre, A. 1981. *After virtue*. Notre Dame, Ind.: University of Notre Dame Press.

MacKinnon, L. K., and D. Miller. 1987. The new epistemology and the Milan approach: Feminist sociopolitical considerations. *Journal of Marital and Family Therapy* 13:139–55.

Madanes, C. 1981. *Strategic family therapy*. San Francisco: Jossey-Bass.

———. 1984. *Behind the one-way mirror: Advances in the practice of strategic therapy*. San Francisco: Jossey-Bass.

Margolin, G. 1982. Ethical and legal considerations in marital and family therapy. *American Psychologist* 37:788–801.

Minuchin, S. 1974. *Families and family therapy*. Cambridge: Harvard University Press.

———. 1984. *Family kaleidoscope*. Cambridge: Harvard University Press.

Minuchin, S., F. Rosman, and L. Baker. 1978. *Psychosomatic families: Anorexia nervosa in context*. Cambridge: Harvard University Press.

Minuchin, S., and H. C. Fishman. 1981. *Family therapy techniques*. Cambridge: Harvard University Press.

Pepper, S. 1944. *World hypotheses*. Berkeley and Los Angeles: University of California Press.

Piercy, F. P., and D. H. Sprenkle. 1983. Ethical, legal and professional issues in family therapy: A graduate level course. *Journal of Marital and Family Therapy* 9, 4:393–402.

Poster, M. 1978. *Critical theory of the family*. New York: Seabury.

Reiss, D. 1981. *The family's construction of reality*. Cambridge: Harvard University Press.

Robinson, D. N. 1976. *An intellectual history of psychology*. New York: Macmillan.

Shorter, E. 1975. *The making of the modern family*. New York: Basic.

Simon, R. ed. 1989. The ethical therapist. [A special issue of the] *Family Therapy Networker* (March/April): 22–47.

Skolnick, A. S., and J. H. Skolnick. *The family in transition.* Glenview, Ill.: Scott, Foresman.

Stout, J. 1988. *Ethics after Babel.* Boston: Beacon Press.

Sullivan, H. S. 1947. *Conceptions of modern psychiatry.* Washington, D. C.: William Alanson White Psychiatric Foundation.

Vande Kemp, H. 1987. Relational ethics in the novels of Charles Williams. *Family Process* 26:283–94.

Wendorf, D. J., and R. J. Wendorf. 1985. A systemic view of family therapy ethics. *Family Process* 24, 4:443–53.

Whitaker, C. 1989. *Midnight musings of a family therapist.* New York: Norton.

Woody, J. D. 1990. Resolving ethical concerns in clinical practice: Toward a pragmatic model. *Journal of Marital and Family Therapy* 16, 2:133–50.

Yoder, J. 1972. *The politics of Jesus.* Philadelphia: Westminster.

Index